TARZAN
MY BODY
CHRISTOPHER COLUMBUS

OTHER BOOKS BY JAIME MANRIQUE

FICTION
El cadáver de papá
Colombian Gold
Latin Moon in Manhattan
Twilight at the Equator
Bésame Mucho: New Gay Latino Fiction (editor)

NON-FICTION
Eminent Maricones: Arenas, Lorca, Puig, and Me

POETRY
Los adoradores de la luna
Scarecow (chapbook)
My Night with Federico García Lorca
Sor Juana's Love Poems (co-translated with Joan Larkin)

CRITICISM
Notas de cine: Confesiones de un crítico amateur

TARZAN
MY BODY
CHRISTOPHER COLUMBUS

by Jaime Manrique

Translated by Margaret Sayers Peden
and Edith Grossman

*For Joel Conarroe,
with my gratitude and best wishes,
Jaime Manrique
June 2001*

Painted Leaf Press
New York City

Published in the United States by Painted Leaf Press, P.O.Box 2480, Times Square Station, New York, NY 10108-2480. Printed in Canada.

Cover design by Les Francoeur
Book design by Brian Brunius

LIBRARY OF CONGRESS CATALOGING-IN-PUBLICATION

Manrique, Jaime, 1949-
    [Tarzan]
    Tarzan ; My body ; Christopher Columbus / by Jaime
    Manrique ; translated by Margaret Sayers Peden and
    Edith Grossman.
        p. cm.
    ISBN 1-891305-57-3
I. Peden, Margaret Sayers. II. Grossman, Edith, 1936- . III.
Manrique, Jaime, 1949- . Mi cuerpo. English. IV. Manrique,
Jaime, 1949- . Cristobal Colon. English. V. Title: Tarzan ;
My body ; Christopher Columbus. VI. Title: My body. VII.
Title: Christopher Columbus. VIII. Title.
    PQ8180.23.A52A227 2001
    861'.64--dc21
                                                2001000473

To Josefina Folgoso

CONTENTS

PART TWO
Tarzan

PART THREE

A Note to the Reader

Though I've lived for over thirty years in the United States, and have written much of my fiction and essays in English, I've continued to write my poetry in Spanish. This book, however, marks a departure for me in the sense that it includes some poems I've recently written in English. Because I'm not certain I'll write many more poems in my stepmother tongue (enough to make a collection of them) in the near future, I've decided to include them in this volume.

Purists will object—and with good reason—that this is not one book but two and a half. The disparate sets of poems I've lumped together span work I've done over a twenty-three-year period: they were begun in youth, and reach all the way into my middle age; they were begun when I saw myself as a Latin American, and reach to a point in my life when I see myself as a Latino—almost an "American."

"Christopher Columbus: Reflections on his Deathbed," written in 1979, was due to be published in 1992 by a small press on the occasion of the 500th anniversary of Christopher Columbus's arrival in the New World, but shortly before we went to press—the poem was already typeset—the publisher closed its operations. Now, it will be appearing five years before the Quincentenary of Christopher Columbus's death in 2006. Reinaldo Arenas's introduction was written shortly before he died in 1990, and though he talks about the poem in terms of the approach of the Quincentenary of the Arrival,

I've decided to leave his words intact. I called the poem a collage because in it I've quoted from several sources, the most obvious being Columbus's *Journals*. In the twenty-three years since the poem was written, I lost my notes. But there are three poets from whose work I borrowed a few lines: Walt Whitman, Leopardi, and Hart Crane.

What surprises me the most is that when I started writing poetry I was under the influence of Anglo-Saxon poets (my early poems owe much to the confessional poets of the sixties and seventies, and "Christopher Columbus" is certainly a poem in the tradition of Browning and Tennyson), yet a quarter of a century later I find myself going back to my roots, Spanish and Latin American poetry—the poetry in my youth I wanted to rebel against. I may have become a gringo after all, but perhaps I've kept writing poems in Spanish—holding on to a language that threatens all the time to get away from me—because at this juncture in my evolution as a poet I would like my poetry to follow in the musical and romantic tradition of San Juan de la Cruz, Neruda, Sor Juana, Borges, Julia de Burgos, Barba Jacob, Silva, Lorca, and Cernuda—the poets whose song is essential to me.

New York
July 2000

TARZAN
MY BODY
CHRISTOPHER COLUMBUS

PART ONE

MI CUERPO / MY BODY

Translations by Margaret Sayers Peden

MI CUERPO

que con mis ojos
abiertos es mi cuerpo
mi cuerpo que con mis ojos
cerrados es perfecto.
Mi cuerpo que cuando lo miran
tus ojos es tu cuerpo.
Mi cuerpo que sólo debió haber
conocido tu cuerpo
que sólo debió haber amado tu cuerpo.
Mi cuerpo que malgasté
en tantos otros cuerpos.
Mi cuerpo sagrado, mi cuerpo
maltratado, mi cuerpo desgastado
y deshecho. Alabado sea el creador
de todos los cuerpos, de mi alabado,
aventurado, dichoso cuerpo.
Mi cuerpo que sólo existe
para tu cuerpo
que ya no es mio
pues ahora es tu cuerpo.
Toma mi cuerpo, te regalo mi cuerpo
bendice con el calor de tus manos mi cuerpo.
Penetra mi cuerpo
devora mi cuerpo
este cuerpo desdichado,
solitario y sediento
mi cuerpo que aulla por tu cuerpo
cuerpo sagrado cuerpo de estiércol
cuerpo que sufrió ser mi cuerpo
cuerpo que gozó
tantos cuerpos ahora yertos
tanta tristeza de tantos cuerpos

MY BODY

which with my eyes
open is my body
my body which with my eyes
closed is perfect.
My body which when your eyes
see it is your body.
My body which should have known
only your body
which should have loved only your body.
My body that I squandered
on so many other bodies.
My sacred body, my mistreated
body, my depleted and exhausted
body. Praise be to the creator
of all bodies, of my praised,
bold and blessed body.
My body that exists only
for your body
that now is not my body
but your body.
Take my body, I give you my body,
bless my body with the warmth of your hands.
Penetrate my body
devour my body
this wretched, lonely,
thirsting body,
my body that howls for your body
sacramental body excremental body
body that suffered being my body
body that pleasured in
so many bodies now stiff and cold
so much sorrow for so many bodies

tantas horas de recuerdos
me ha regalado mi cuerpo
tantas delicias que me proporcionaron
miles de cuerpos
ese regalo sagrado que nos hace sólo el cuerpo.
Este poema es un regalo
de tu cuerpo y mi cuerpo.

so many hours of memories
my body has given me
so much happiness thousands of bodies
have provided me
that sacred gift only the body gives us.
This poem is a gift
from your body and my body.

POEMA DE OTOñO

Hay un río detrás de la casa.
Desde la ventana de mi cuarto
abajo, en la hondonada,
a través del abigarrado
ropaje del bosque,
aparece el río en el otoño
a medida que el mundo
se desnuda y los espacios
se abren. Entonces,
veo una rodaja
del río—un espejo
que refleja los colores del cielo
y también las estrellas.
De repente, después
de una orgía de colores
y el cataclismo de octubre
cuando las hojas encendidas
se desprenden como una tempestad
de mariposas, las noches
invitan a la contemplación,
las estrellas son flores diminutas
puntos tan imperceptibles
que parecen una creación de mis ojos.
Así también es la poesía—nace
en la imaginación, en el tránsito
del despertar al ensueño.
Mis poemas brotan
no para reflejar al mundo
sino para transcenderlo.
Este otoño no he pensado en la muerte
sino en ti, mi amado.
Pues a medida que el mundo

AUTUMN POEM

There is a river behind my house.
From the window of my room,
below, in the ravine,
through the motley
clothing of the woods,
a river appears in autumn
as the world
grows bare and spaces
open. Then
I see a slice
of the river—a mirror
reflecting the colors of the sky
and then the stars.
Suddenly, after
an orgy of color
and the cataclysm of October
when the blazing leaves
are released like a storm
of butterflies, the nights
invite contemplation,
the stars are tiny
points so dimly seen
they seem an invention of my eyes.
My poetry is like that—born
of the imagination, in the passage
from waking to dream.
My poems come to life
not to reflect the world
but to transcend it.
This autumn I've not thought of death
but of you, my love.
For in the way the world

se desnuda y queda
expuesto a los elementos
—como los árboles desnudos—
el milagro del amor
también nos hace vulnerables.

grows bare and is
exposed to the elements
—like the denuded trees—
the miracle of love
makes us, too, vulnerable.

LLAMADAS QUE NO LLEGAN

Esas llamadas
cuando espero con el aliento
entrecortado, el corazón
suspendido
sobre un abismo oscuro.
No pido sino escuchar
tu voz
para que se abran todas las puertas
y ventanas y aires cálidos y frescos
ventilen mis recintos mustios;
no pido sino sostenerte
desnudo
en mis brazos, mis labios adorando
tu piel
que me alimenta.

Esos días interminables
cuando no me llamas
cuando ignoras el efecto
que una palabra tuya,
cualquier palabra,
tendría para apaciguar mi angustia.

El amor me ha arrancado
de la roca a la cual me aferraba
y me lanza hacia
un vacío
donde caigo convertido en piedra.
Porque cuando no escucho tu voz
aún tus mentiras
aún tu indiferencia
no puedo, no quiero

CALLS THAT NEVER COME

Those calls
I wait for
with my heart in my throat,
my head swimming
above a dark abyss.
All I ask is to hear
your voice
so all the doors and windows
will open and warm, fresh air
will sweep out all my sadness;
all I ask is
to hold you
in my arms,
my lips adoring
your skin,
which is my sustenance.

Those interminable days
when you don't call,
when you are heedless of the effect that
one word from you,
any word,
would have in soothing my anguish.

Love has torn me from
the rock I was clinging to
and hurled me toward
a void
where I am falling turned to stone.

Because when I don't hear your voice
even your lies

continuar
pues me he transformado
en roca.

Aún así,
con mis versos
quisiera hacerte inmortal
para que la historia te recuerde
como la mayor fuente de placer
que ha conocido el hombre.

Cuando te sonrojas
intimas mareadas planetarias
que comprometen
el equilibrio
de la tierra;
y con sólo una mirada
una caricia tuya
se hunde el suelo bajo mis pies
creando terremotos
arrasadores
pues eres un Dios
cruel como un Dios
sordo a mis plegarias
indiferente a mis dichas.
Y sin embargo,
te adoro
pues aún el amor no correspondido
es preferible a tu ausencia.
Yemayá, Diosa del Mar y los Amores,
cúrame de este amor,
de esta ponzoña.

even your indifference
I can't, I don't want to
go on
because you have transformed me
and I am become rock.

Even so
I have wanted
to make you immortal with my poems
so that history would remember you
as the greatest font of pleasure
man has ever known.

When you smile
you hint at dizzying planetary waves
that compromise
the equlibrium
of the earth, and with only one look
one caress from you
the ground sinks beneath my feet
creating devastating
earthquakes,
for you are a god
cruel as a god
deaf to my pleas
indifferent to my words
and yet
I adore you,
for even love you don't return
is preferable to your absence.
O Yemayá, goddess of the sea and passion,
cure me of this love,
this poison.

POEMA PARA TI

Todo en la naturaleza existe
antes que tú y yo existiéramos,
pero estas líneas no existirían sin ti.

Este mes de julio,
con sus tardes lánguidas, hirvientes
y noches escarchadas de diamante,
la vida misma parece detenerse;
el ruiseñor vespertino
con la brevedad de su canto
me recuerda que mi juventud perece,
y que un día, tú también,
perderás tu lozanía.

Estas tardes estivales
los girasoles me recuerdan
el oropel de tus cabellos,
y no hay agua tan clara ni tan prístina
como la luz líquida de tus pupilas.

Estos días de julio
con su desgarro de pasión empozada
tienen tu sello;
y el último deshojar de mi juventud
siempre resplandecerá con tu recuerdo.

POEM FOR YOU

Everything in nature existed
before you and I existed,
but these lines would not exist without you.

This month, July,
with its languid, sultry afternoons
and diamond-frosted nights,
life itself seems to stop;
with the brevity of its song
the twilight's nightingale
reminds me that my youth is ending
and that one day you, too,
will lose your bloom.

These summer afternoons
the sunflowers remind me
of the glints of gold in your hair,
and there is no water as clear or pure
as the liquid light of your eyes.

These July days
with their rending buried passion
have your name burned on them;
and your memory will always cast its glow
on the last unfolding of my youth.

POEMA DEL INSTANTE

En este instante
en algún lugar del mundo
alguien se despierta
a la embriaguez del amor.
Una mano lo acaricia
y lo convierte en un tejido
de venas que son ríos de sangre;
siente su corazón
abrirse, una semilla seca
que germina en el delta de su cuerpo.

En este instante surcaría
los cielos catrópticos
de esta ciudad de vidrio y acero
donde nuestros vulnerables
corazones—torpes músculos
donde residen el sueño, la ternura—
luchan para no hundirse
en la desolación del no querer
que es la nada.

En este instante
sueño con ese momento
cuando tú me tocarás de nuevo
y cerraré los ojos
y volaré por un cielo nocturno
donde los astros y los planetas
brillen con luces que, al tocarnos,
nos transformarán en ámbar
de fulgor inaudito.

En este instante

POEM FOR THIS INSTANT

This instant
somewhere in the world
someone is waking up
to the intoxication of love.
A hand is caressing him
turning him into a network
of veins that are rivers of blood;
he feels his heart
opening, a dry seed
germinating in the delta of his body.

This instant I would be
scoring the mirrored sky
of this city of glass and steel
in which our vulnerable
hearts—clumsy muscles
housing dreams and tenderness—
are struggling to keep from sinking
into the desolation of not loving
that is nothingness.

This instant
I am dreaming of the moment
when you will touch me again
and I will close my eyes
and fly through the night sky
in which stars and planets
shine with a light that as it touches us
transforms us into an amber
of improbable splendor.

This instant

en la cara oscura de la tierra
un enamorado sueña
con su amado
un gato con una paloma
un niño con la llave
que abrirá la puerta de la fantasía
y lo convertirá en poeta.

En este instante nadie
sueña con guerras, ni cataclismos.
En este instante
alguien rompe
las cadenas opresoras
y al despertarse notará que le brotaron
alas en el sueño y volará a otros
mundos de colores de selva.

En este instante, mi amado,
no sabes que pienso en ti.
¿Y si nunca lo supieras?
Está bien, porque en este instante
te tengo atrapado en mi poema.

on the dark face of the earth
a lover is dreaming of
his loved one
a cat of a dove
a boy of a key
that will open the door of fantasy
and make him a poet.

This instant no one
is dreaming of wars or cataclysms.
This instant
someone is breaking
oppressive chains
and on waking will find that in his sleep
he sprouted wings, and he will fly to other
worlds the colors of lush jungle.

This instant, my beloved,
you do not know I am thinking of you.
And if you never find that out?
It doesn't matter, because this instant
I have trapped you in my poem.

AL ERA DE ALABAMA

Al era de Alabama
lo conocí en una laguna mental,
en un bar del Greenwich Village.
Al despertarme por la mañana
Al estaba sentado
en mi cama, leyendo un libro de Pauline Kael.
Resultó ser que compartíamos varios amigos.

Al trabajaba en la Biblioteca Pública
de Brooklyn, había leído más libros
que cualquier otra persona que yo había conocido
y, aunque era gago, podía hablar
acerca de su libros favoritos con una pasión
que me fascinaba.

Tuvimos una breve relación sexual.
Al vivía con David y yo con Bill.
Estábamos a finales de los años setenta
y la promiscuidad era la norma.
Además de ver a Al, yo veía a Walter,
Nicol y a Neil. Los tres eran
rubios y amaban los libros. Los tres
me obsequiaban novelas, poemarios.
Al sacó de la Biblioteca de Broooklyn
los *Diarios* de Dorothy Wordsworth
que conservo hasta hoy día.

Cuando Al se dio cuenta de que además
de vivir con Bill me acostaba con Walter y Nicol
(El también los conocía) dejamos
de acostarnos. En esos días,
muchas relaciones duraban

AL WAS FROM ALABAMA

Al was from Alabama.
I met him during a mental blackout
in a bar in Greenwich Village.
When I woke up the next morning
Al was sitting
on my bed reading a book by Pauline Kael.
It turned out we had several friends in common.

Al worked in the Brooklyn
Public Library; he had read more books
than any person I had ever known
and, even though he stuttered, he could talk
about his favorite books with a passion
I found fascinating.

We had a brief fling.
Al was living with David, and I was with Bill.
It was the end of the seventies
and promiscuity was the norm.
Besides seeing Al, I was involved with Walter,
Nicol, and Neil. All three were
blond, and they all loved books. All three
showered me with novels and books of poems.
Al checked out from the Brooklyn Library
a copy of Dorothy Wordsworth's *Diaries*
that I have to this day.

When Al learned that besides living with
Bill I was also sleeping with Walter and Nicol
(he knew them, too) he called a stop to
our affair. In those days
relationships lasted only for weeks,

semanas, días y con frecuencia horas.
Terminamos de amigos aunque existía
en el fondo un cierto resquemor
(el resquemor de aquéllos que se han compartido
sexualmente, amándose por un instante).

Unos cuantos años después, Al cayó
enfermo de Sida. Para esa época
había dejado de beber
y ahora tenía una serenidad,
una sabiduría que no tenía nada
que ver con los libros. Un día
Al me dijo: "Es ridículo decir
que le estoy agradecido a AA por salvarme
la vida. Agradecimiento es una palabra
inadecuada para describir ese milagro".

Unos pocos días antes de su muerte
fui a visitarlo, pues Al necesitaba
ayuda. Era una tarde lluviosa
de abril y encontré a Al en la sala
de su apartamento—las uñas de sus pies
largas, arqueadas, amarillentas—un olor
apestoso emanaba de su boca. Al
me pidió que le hiciera varias
diligencias: comprarle comida
china, ciertas medicinas que necesitaba.

Al estaba próximo a la muerte.
Algo extraño, aún sublime, había ocurrido:
a pesar de su apariencia de monstruo,
de su mal genio (le había traído algo diferente
de lo que me había pedido),
Al se había convertido
en una apariencia luminosa, trascendental

sometimes days, frequently, only hours.
We ended as friends, although deep down
there was a hint of edginess between us
(the uneasiness of people who have shared
sex, made love for a brief while).

A few years later, Al fell
victim to AIDS. By that time
he had stopped drinking
and had acquired a serenity,
a wisdom, that had nothing
to do with his books. One day
Al said to me: "It's silly to say
I'm grateful to AA for having saved
my life. Gratitude is a poor
word for describing that miracle."

A few days before Al's death
I went to see him because he needed
help. It was a rainy April
afternoon, and I found Al in the living room
of his apartment; his toenails were long,
curved, yellowed, and his breath
was foul. Al asked me
to run several errands for him:
bring him some Chinese food
and buy certain medicines he needed.

Al was near death.
Something strange, even sublime, had happened.
Despite his appalling appearance,
his terrible mood (I had brought something other
than what he had asked for),
Al had become
luminous and transcendent

(furioso por la brevedad de su vida),
se había transformado en una llama radiante, pura.

Ver tal transformación en un ser humano,
en alguien al borde de la muerte,
era un gran privilegio, algo
que también me transformaba.
Ahora, cuando pienso en Al
así es como me gusta recordarlo.
Al murió en abril, uno más
entre los miles que han muerto de Sida.

(raging at the brevity of his life),
he was transformed into a radiant, pure flame.

To see such a transformation in a human being,
in someone on the verge of death,
was a great privilege, something
that transformed me as well.
Now when I think of Al
that is how I like to remember him.
Al died in April, one more
among the thousands who have died of AIDS.

TURISMO

Esta noche, en Canaima,
las estrellas brillan
muy bajas, lejos de las luces
del mundo occidental.
Detrás del monte que circunda el campamento
la luna brilla y su resplandor
se levanta desde la selva profunda
como si fuera una cancha de tenis
con sus luces encendidas.

A la medianoche
los cráteres de la luna se pueden
ver con toda claridad,
su luz tan clara
como la de una tarde
lluviosa y argentosa de Manhattan
cuando el mundo
es un film en blanco en negro.

Esta selva es una monstruosidad.
Hay más cataratas en Canaima
que en todas las naciones europeas.

He llegado a esa encrucijada
de mi vida en la cual
todos los caminos desembocan
en el turismo.
Esta necesidad
de ver, comprobar, es una fiebre
contagiosa.

En esta región añorada

TRAVEL

Tonight, in Canaima,
the stars are ablaze and low
in the sky, far from the lights
of the Western world.
Behind the trees that encircle the camp
the moon is shining, its radiance
making the deep jungle glow
as if it were a tennis court
flooded with light.

At midnight
the craters of the moon
are clearly visible
and the moonlight is as bright
as that of a rainy, silvery Manhattan
afternoon
when the world
is a black-and-white film.

This jungle is awe-inspiring.
There are more waterfalls in Canaima
than in all the European nations combined.

I have come to this intersection
in my life where
all roads lead
to travel.

This need
to taste, to see for oneself,
is a contagious fever.

explotada
murió mi tío Hernán
cuando su avión
detonó
sobre la selva y sólo
su mano fue encontrada por mi tía.
Yo también reconocería las manos
de todos los hombres que he amado,
como reconozco en la oscuridad
la mano de Michael, el hombre
a quien amo.
El tiene la fiebre
del Vih
y yo tengo una relación con él
y con su virus—
el triángulo del milenio.

En esta Canaima
donde todo es desbordamiento
vegetal y mineral,
el ser humano perece más
que cualquier otra forma de vida.

Esta noche, desde esta terraza,
en la mitad de la selva oscura de la vida
agradezco al turismo por traerme
hasta aquí a esta Capilla Sixtina vegetal,
este Lourdes milagroso, a revisitar
el pasado y el presente
de la muerte que circunda
en esta morada del amor y del éxtasis.

In this fondly remembered,
exploited land
died my uncle Hernán,
his airplane
blew up
over the jungle and only
his hand was recovered by my aunt.
I know I would recognize the hands
of all the men I have loved,
as even in the dark I recognize
the hand of Michael, the man
I love.
He is HIV
positive
and I have a relationship with him
and with his virus—
this milennium's triangle.

Here in Canaima
where everything is vegetal
and mineral excess
the human being is more
vulnerable than any other life form.

Tonight, from this terrace,
in the middle of the dark jungle of life
I am grateful to travel for bringing me
here to nature's Sistine Chapel,
this miraculous Lourdes, to revisit
the past and the present
of the death that surrounds us
in this sanctuary of love and ecstasy.

VIAJE EN TREN AL CAER LA NOCHE

Como miel ahumada
la noche desciende sobre el paisaje
y su oscuridad lo impregna todo.
La luna cuelga en el cielo
redonda, plateada, un punto de referencia
sobre las distancias que el tren devora.
Nubes claras pasan enfrente de la luna;
pensamientos cruzan mi memoria,
interponiéndose entre tú y yo
como la noche se interpone
entre la luna y el paisaje y este secreto
es la única sorpresa de este viaje.
La realidad se ha tornado monótona
como la geografía en la oscuridad.
Esta noche viajamos juntos—
esta es la jornada de regreso.
El tren nos lleva de vuelta a nuestro hogar
a los sueños que soñaremos en nuestro lecho.
La noche nos lleva de regreso
a ese momento en el cual nuestros cuerpos
se acoplen el uno al otro
como el clavo a la pared, el marco al cuadro.
Ahora, junto a ti, sólo sé esto:
la misión de la noche es la de expandirse
a través del continente;
la del tren, conducir a los viajeros;
la de la luna, iluminar el espectáculo;
y la de la nube... ¿pero no es acaso la nube
el pensamiento que se interpone
en nuestros cuerpos?
y ¿no es el pensamiento, lo que separa
el día con mis incertidumbres
de la noche en la cual te amo demasiado?

TRAIN TRIP AT NIGHTFALL

Like smoky honey
night spills over the countryside
as its darkness seeps into the ground.
The moon hangs in the sky
round, silvery, a point of reference
above the distances devoured by the train.
Bright clouds pass before the moon;
thoughts cross through my memory,
filling the space between you and me
the way the night fills the space
between moon and countryside
and awareness of this secret
is the journey's one surprise.
Reality has become monotonous
like the landscape in the dark.
Tonight we are traveling together—
this is a journey of return.
The train is carrying us home, back
to dreams we will dream in our own bed.
Night is carrying us back
to that moment when our bodies
are coupled one with the other,
like the nail in the wall, the picture in the frame.
Now, beside you, this is all I know:
the mission of night is to spread
across the continent;
that of the train, to carry travelers;
that of the moon, to illuminate the panorama;
and that of the cloud...but isn't the cloud
a thought filtering
into our bodies?
And isn't thought what separates
day, with my uncertainty,
from night, when I love you too much?

LA RUTA DESCONOCIDA DE AMHERST

Una tarde de colores otoñales
pasé por enfrente de la casa
de la bella de Amherst
y unas cuadras más adelante
la calle se convirtió
en una carretera que cruzaba
prados, bosques y montañas.
Detuve el coche para recoger un hermoso
muchacho rumbo a las montañas
violáceas en la distancia. Cargaba
una pequeña mochila
y viajaba para observar los colores.

Yo no vivía en dirección de la montaña
sino hacia el norte helado
en una cabaña con un río en la hondonada
detrás de la casa donde mis visitantes
más frecuentes eran Jake, un perro
pastor alemán, que cuando ponía
sus patas delanteras en mis hombros,
era tan alto como un oso. Su lengua
cálida y áspera me lamía con el vigor
y cariño torpe de un adolescente.
Mis otros visitantes eran una familia
de pavos, veinte o treinta pavos salvajes,
que volaban desde la colina de mi casa
por encima del camino y caían
estrepitosamente en el bosque, bultos
alados rellenos de plumas.

Han pasado algunos años desde ese otoño.
Ya no vivo en Amherst

THE AMHERST ROAD UNTAKEN

One autumn-colored afternoon
I drove past the house
of the Belle of Amherst;
a few blocks farther on
the street became
a highway crossing through
meadows, woods, and mountains.
I stopped the car to pick up a handsome
boy heading toward the lavender
mountains in the distance. He was wearing
a small back-pack
and was on his way to see the colors.

I didn't live in the direction of the mountain
but toward the icy north,
in a cabin with a river in the ravine
behind it where my most frequent
visitors were Jake, a German
sheperd, who when he put his
front paws on my shoulders
was as tall as a bear. His rough
warm tongue licked me with the vigor
and clumsy affection of a teenager.
My other visitors were a family
of turkeys, twenty or thirty wild turkeys,
who would fly from the hill of my house
over the road to light
noisily in the woods, winged
pillows filled with feathers.

Several years have gone by since that autumn.
I no longer live in Amherst

y ese muchacho que recogí
ahora ya debe de ser un hombre. Nunca
recorrí la carretera hacia
esas montañas aunque siempre quise hacerlo.
Hoy es un día de otoño en Nueva York
y de esta estación febril
sólo puedo apreciar la dulce luz
acariciando los edificios del alto Manhattan.
La casa donde vivió Emily Dickinson
todavía está allí y la cabaña
donde viví estará ocupada por otro poeta.
Jake, el perro lobo, se habrá sosegado
con el paso de los años
y la familia de pavos salvajes
habrá sobrevivido otra estación violenta.
Hoy pienso en ese muchacho
y me lo imagino todavía en el bosque en busca
de colores exaltados, como yo los busco
en este bosque de cemento donde habito,
donde anhelo esa pura exaltación que sólo producen
los colores delirantes de la estación
que es un frágil puente
entre la vida de colores exaltados
y el blancor de la muerte.

and that boy to whom I gave a ride
must be a man by now. I never
took that highway toward
the mountain, though I always wanted to.
Today is an autumn day in New York
and of this feverish season
I cherish only the gentle light
caressing the buildings of upper Manhattan.
The house where Emily Dickinson lived
is still there, and the cabin
where I lived is occupied by another poet.
Jake, the sheperd, will have settled down
with the passing of the years
and the family of wild turkeys
will have survived another harsh season.
Today I think of that boy
and imagine him still in the woods looking
for vibrant colors, the way I look for them
in the forest of cement that is my home,
where I yearn for that pure exaltation that comes only
from the delirious colors of the season
that is a fragile bridge
between the life of vibrant colors
and the bleached landscape of death.

LUIS CERNUDA EN SOUTH HADLEY

para Manuel Ulacia

Una noche de pavor nocturno
termina. Afuera
en el amanecer Yankee
todo está congelado
y la oscuridad no cederá
por horas. Afuera
todo está
en tinieblas y pienso
llamar a un amigo
en otro continente
donde ya es de día,
donde las horas
en las cuales somos
ventrílocuos de los muertos
han cedido a la claridad del día.
Pienso llamar a un lugar
donde los seres despiertos
hayan sacudido
los sueños en los cuales
todavía estoy inmerso.
Todo lo que tengo que hacer
es levantar la bocina
y marcar París, Madrid, Londres
—ciudades oscuras donde el sol
brilla ahora—hasta que recuerdo
que Sally, Severo y Luis
están muertos
que sus voces
ya no podrán aliviar
la angustia de estas noches
cuando le pertenezco

LUIS CERNUDA IN SOUTH HADLEY

For Manuel Ulacia

The dark hours of night terrors
have passed. Outside
in the Yankee dawn
everything is frozen
and it will be hours before
night fully surrenders. Outside
everything lies
in darkness and I'm thinking
of calling a friend
on a different continent
where there is still daylight,
where the hours in which we are
ventriloquists for the dead
have yielded to the clarity of day.
I'm thinking of calling a place
where wide-awake people
have shaken off
the dreams in which
I am still immersed.
All I have to do is
lift the receiver
and dial Paris, Madrid, London
-dark cities where the sun
is shining brightly-but then I remember
that Sally, Severo, and Luis
are all dead,
remember that their voices
can no longer ease
the anguish of these nights
when I am captive
to my ghosts.

a mis fantasmas.
Entonces pienso
no en los muertos lejanos,
sus cenizas diluidas;
pienso en Luis Cernuda,
solitario,
amargado
por un sueño
destruido.
Cernuda,
aquí en South Hadley,
hasta que finalmente
puedo verlo
caminando por la calle blanca.
Había terminado la Segunda Guerra Mundial.
Al principio le extrañaba
que los cielos cenicientos de Europa
y los ríos sangrientos
de España no existieran aquí
donde la naturaleza era prístina.
Y lo veo también en las noches
de invierno sentado cerca a un fuego,
leyendo, ensimismado,
mientras masivas nevadas sellaban
los caminos a Northampton, a Amherst
donde posiblemente vivía otro poeta
exiliado, pero especialmente
la ruta de Amherst, donde Emily Dickinson
había vivido una vida
en la cual la poesía
era la vida.
En esas noches mudas de South Hadley
en las cuales sólo eran audibles
las pisadas de los fantasmas
lejos, muy lejos

Then I think
not about my distant dead,
their diluted ashes,
I think about Luis Cernuda,
alone,
embittered
by a destroyed
dream.
Cernuda,
here in South Hadley,
until finally
I can see him
walking down the white street.
The Second World War was over.
At first he was dumbfounded
not to find the ashen skies
and bloody rivers of Europe here
where nature was still pristine.
I also see him on winter
nights, sitting beside the fire,
reading, absorbed in his thoughts,
as heavy snowfalls block
the roads to Norhthampton, to Amherst
where maybe another exiled poet
lived, but especially
the road to Amherst, where Emily Dickinson
had lived a life
in which poetry
was life.
On those muted nights in South Hadley
when nothing could be heard but
the footsteps of distant
ghosts far
from any human warmth,
Cernuda learned to conquer his terror,

de todo calor humano,
Cernuda aprendió a domar su terror,
a desnudarse completamente
hasta que sólo su alma
hablaba, hasta que un día,
como Lázaro, intuyó un calor de luz,
sintió su corazón latir
por la tibieza del perfume de las lilas
fluyendo en sus venas
y decidió regresar al sol,
al colorido de México
que lo llamaba como una sirena.
Con sus ojos
apagados tanto tiempo
por las tinieblas de la historia,
por las frígidas noches
invernales de South Hadley
donde el mundo era un purgatorio
de fuego blanco,
Luis Cernuda levantó vuelo.
Entonces, en su edad otoñal,
por un instante breve
pero eterno, encontró
por primera vez el amor,
escribió sus mejores poemas de pasión
y murió la muerte
triunfal de los grandes poetas.

to strip himself bare,
until only his soul
spoke...until one day,
like Lazarus, he sensed the heat of light,
he felt his heart beat
with the warmth of the lilacs' perfume
flowing through his veins,
and he decided to go back to the sun,
to the color of Mexico
that called to him like a siren.
With eyes
clouded so long
by the darkness of history,
by the frigid winter
nights of South Hadley
where the world was a purgatory
of white fire,
Luis Cernuda took flight.
Then, in his autumn years,
for a brief but eternal
instant, he found
love for the first time,
he wrote his best poems of passion
and he died the triumphal
death of great poets.

VARIACIÓN SOBRE UN TEMA DE HART CRANE

Han pasado muchos años desde que vi
tantas estrellas. Desde aquí,
la oscura tierra, las observo rodeado
de altos pinos negros, guardas y testigos
de los secretos de la noche. Hace años,
cuando prefería la compañía
de las ilusiones, deseaba saber sus nombres
como anhelaba conocer mi destino (los cielos
eran entonces un cristal para predecir el futuro).

Las cosas me han sucedido, aunque no
como yo las esperaba. La noche
es tibia, y entre los pinos
y la alta hierba, se esconde una mofeta temerosa,
su apestoso efluvio penetra mis sentidos
y ese olor agridulce punza mi corazón
como lo punzan esta noche las estrellas.

Ahora soy un hombre más cerca
del fin que del principio,
ahora me consuelo con saber que esta noche
las estrellas que veo son las mismas
que sedujeron a mis abuelos y a mis padres
y su fulgor es el brillo de sus ilusiones
esculpidas en diamante.

Lejos de la ciudad, en esta quietud de sombras,
he llegado a una encrucijada en el bosque.
Uno conduce a la casa, la otra es una invitación
al bosque profundo donde alces, mofetas y lechuzas
me esperan. Años atrás habría escogido
el camino del bosque. Ahora, me encamino hacia la luz

VARIATION ON A THEME OF HART CRANE

It has been years since I saw
so many stars. From here,
the dark earth, I see them encircled
by tall black pines, guards and witnesses
of the night's secrets. Years past,
when I preferred the company
of illusions, I wanted to learn their names,
as I longed to know my destiny (the skies then
were a crystal ball for predicting the future).

Things have happened to me, though not
the way I expected. The night
is warm, and a timid skunk
is hiding among the pines and high grass,
its powerful stench penetrates my senses
and the pungent, sweetish odor pierces my heart
the way the stars pierce the night.

Now I am a man closer to
the end than the beginning,
and it comforts me to know that
the stars I see tonight are the same
that seduced my grandparents and my parents,
and this glory is the splendor of their dreams
sculpted in diamonds.

Far from the city, in these quiet shadows
I have come to a crossroads in the woods.
One road leads to my house, the other is an invitation
to the deep forest where elk, skunks, and owls
await. Years ago I would have chosen
the road into the woods. Now I walk toward the light

de la casa, pues las estrellas esta noche son una invitación
a escribir estos versos; y las preguntas que antes ellas
me inspiraban, ahora sé que no tienen respuesta.

of the house, for tonight the stars are an invitation
to write these lines, and I have learned that
the questions they once evoked have no answers.

TU ARTE INMACULADO, BILLIE HOLIDAY

En el hospital Metropolitano,
el 17 de julio de 1955,
a los cuarenta y cuatro años de edad,
la voz destruída,
encadenada a tu lecho,
tus ojos dos algas negras fosforescentes,
las narices taponeadas de heroína,
los sueños perfumados de gardenias,
cantaste tu último blues.

Todos los poetas están de acuerdo, Billie,
el día de tu muerte
se instaló perennemente la tristeza.

En tu repertorio
frutos extraños cuelgan
de los árboles sureños—
negros linchados bajo cielos sangrientos.
Tanta crueldad nunca fue tan bien cantada.
De tus labios los sonidos
salen purificados. En tu vocabulario
todo sonido es sacro.
Después de escucharte, Billie,
emergimos pálidos, envejecidos,
desolados para siempre.

BILLIE HOLIDAY: IMMACULATE ART

In the Metropolitan Hospital,
on July 17, 1955,
at the age of forty-four
voice destroyed,
chained to your bed,
eyes two black, phosphorescent algae,
nostrils clogged by heroin,
dreams perfumed with gardenia,
you sang your last *blues*.

No poet disagrees, Billie,
the day you died
sadness moved in for good.

In your repertoire
strange fruit hangs
from southern trees:
blacks lynched beneath bloody skies.
So much cruelty was never sung so well,
Sound issues purified
from your lips. In your vocabulary
every note is sacred.
After hearing you, Billie,
we walk away pale, aged,
forever desolate.

DESPUÉS DE ESCUCHAR "LA SONATA DE KREUTZER"

Pozdnischeff atraviesa la campiña nevada
el aire un es tónico
el camino es parejo y hermoso
la escarchada mañana otoñal
brilla asoleada.
Arropado en el trineo,
las primeras notas de "La sonata de Kreutzer"
no le elevan ni le deprimen
el alma a Pozdnischeff—
le parecen simplemente absurdas.
Los celos lo enceguecen
escucha demonios en vez de notas.
Sus ojos húmedos, febriles,
ven la expresión plácida, sonriente
de su mujer y el amante
cuando terminan de tocar la sonata.
Y Pozdnischeff, quien teme el ridículo,
abraza la destrucción de la locura.

Más tarde, lo enardece
la resistencia del cuello de su esposa
y de un golpe
le entierra la daga
en el costado izquierdo.
Nunca olvidará el crujido del corsé,
el cuchillo desgarrando
las membranas
ni el gesto de ella empuñando la daga
para ayudarlo, cuando Podznischeff
intenta sacar el cuchillo
para deshacer el daño.

UPON HEARING THE "KREUTZER" SONATA

Pozdnischeff is riding through snow-covered fields
the air is a tonic
the road is smooth and beautiful
the frosty autumn morning
sparkles in the sun.
Bundled up in the sleigh, Pozdnischeff
hears the first notes of the "Kreutzer" sonata,
they neither elevate nor afflict
his soul,
they merely strike him as absurd.
Blinded with jealousy
he hears demons instead of notes.
His watery, feverish eyes
see the placid, smiling expression
of his wife and her lover
as the sonata comes to an end.
And Pozdnischeff, who fears ridicule,
embraces the annihilation of madness.

Later, his rage is kindled
by his wife's unyielding neck
and with one thrust
he drives the dagger
into her left side.
He will never forget the crunch of her corset,
of the knife ripping
membrane
nor forget her grasping the hilt
to help, when Pozdnischeff
tries to pull out the dagger
to undo the harm done.

Cuando visita a su esposa
en el lecho de muerte,
el rostro rasguñado, hinchado,
la nariz ensangrentada, le repugnan.
Años después, Pozdnischeff
viajará en trenes por la campiña rusa
y se estremecerá al recordar
ese momento en el trineo
cuando intuyó su mal en los primeros
acordes de "La sonata de Kreutzer".
Tampoco olvidará, y se estremecerá
aún más al recordar,
la expresión de su esposa
quien, al expirar,
en un gesto agónico final
lo mira con una expresión cruel, fría,
de odio infinito.

When he visits his wife
on her death bed,
her swollen, lacerated face
and bloody nose repel him.
Years later, Pozdnischeff
will often travel across Russia by train
and he will shudder when he recalls
that moment in the sleigh
when he had a premonition of evil
with the first chords of the "Kreutzer" sonata.
Neither will he forget—and he will shiver
convulsively at the memory—
the expression of his wife
who, as she died,
with her last dying breath
pierces him with a cruel cold look
of infinite loathing.

NOCTURNO EN GREENWICH VILLAGE

Esta noche veo la luna
como la ven esos artistas que han explotado
el perfil de una mujer de nariz respingada,
pómulos salientes y ojeras que son mares de sombra.

¿Será posible que si miramos algo
desprevenidamente, veamos finalmente el cliché
que siempre hemos despreciado;
será posible que el misterio
de las cosas sea tan fácil de descifrar?

Ahora la luna creciente es el rostro
de una mujer preñada de luz,
una Mona Lisa celeste, demacrada
por demasiadas vigilias nocturnas.

En el muelle sobre el Río Hudson,
recostados contra las vallas metálicas,
hay parejas de hombres
entrelazados acariciándose delicadamente,
sus caricias una expresión del amor mismo.

Esta noche los hombres
en el muelle son sólo amantes
celebrando su amor bajo la
tutela de la luna. Y esa paloma blanca
que vuela hacia el cielo uvado es
el amor mismo, no el cliché de afiches turísticos;
es la pureza de todo lo que sólo aspira
a existir bajo un cielo sin nubes, diáfano, donde
el rostro de la luna es un ancla de luz y el cielo
una manta que nos cobijará cuando anochezca.

NOCTURNE: GREENWICH VILLAGE

Tonight I see the moon
pictured by those artists who have exploited
the profile of a woman with a pug nose, round cheeks
and eyes with deep circles like seas of shadow.

Is it possible that if we look at something
in a new light we finally will see the cliché
we have always scorned?
Can it be possible that the mystery
of things is that easy to decipher?

Now the waxing moon is the face
of a woman gravid with light,
a celestial Mona Lisa wearied
by too many night vigils.

On the pier by the Hudson River,
backs against the iron fence,
couples embrace, men
gently stroking one another,
their caresses the face of love itself.

Tonight those men
on the pier are simply
lovers celebrating their love beneath
the tutelage of the moon. And the white dove
lifting toward a grape-plump sky
is love, not the cliché of tourism posters;
it is the purity of all that seeks nothing more
than to live beneath a clear and cloudless sky where
the face of the moon is an anchor of light and the sky
a mantle that will cover us when night falls.

REMOLCADOR

era una de esas palabras
que odiaba en mi niñez.
Otras eran corisa, astromelia,
palabras usadas por los Ardilas—
el clan de mi madre.
Me parecían palabras torpes,
vulgares—palabras de campesinos.

Esta mañana de verano
briosa, azulada, mientras caminaba
enfrente de la Universidad de Columbia
recordé la palabra
remolcador... brotó
de mis labios, un suspiro
que se desvaneció hacia el alto Manhattan.

Es curioso como en días amables
camino hasta el parque,
me siento en un banco a observar
el Hudson, como en otras épocas
contemplaba el Río Magdalena.

Hace diez años, en Santa Marta,
una noche caminando el malecón
encontré una muchedumbre alrededor
de un templete, donde unos estudiantes
entonaban coplas desgarradas
acerca del agonizante
Río Magdalena.

Estaba solo. Era una noche clara
sobre la bahía. El mar

REMOLCADOR,

tugboat, was one of those words
I despised as a child.
Others were *corisa* and *astromelia*,
words used by the Ardilas—
my mother's clan.
I thought they were commonplace-
country people's words.

This breezy blue summer
morning, as I was walking past
Columbia University
I remembered the word
remolcador—it sprang
from my lips, a sigh
that floated off toward upper Manhattan.

It's curious how on pleasant days
I walk to the park
and sit on a bench to look at
the Hudson, the way in other days
I watched the Río Magdalena.

Ten years ago, in Santa Marta,
walking one night along the breakwater
I ran into a crowd gathered around
a platform where students
were reciting emotional poems about the dying
Río Magdalena.

I was alone. The night sky
was clear over the bay. The sea
was funereal silk

era una seda mortuoria
y su frescor me acariciaba.
Tenía treinta y siete años;
era un hombre maduro.
Ahora, una década más tarde
pienso en esos jóvenes y sus coplas
y siento el dolor y la nostagia
que ellos sentían.

El remolcador era una cosa
grande, ocre, metálica
que se desplazaba lentamente
por las aguas cenagosas del Magdalena.
Cargaba tambores de gasolina, jeeps,
ganado, costales repletos de cocos secos.
No era una cosa hermosa.
Pero mi familia pronunciaba
la palabra remolcador—
un lazo entre el pueblo y el mundo de afuera—
con una reverencia casi religiosa.

Es curioso cómo he pasado
gran parte de mi vida
en ciudades ribereñas;
cómo el río acabó convirtiéndose
en mi destino
aunque ahora, cuando veo
un remolcador surcar el Hudson—
una cosa fea, un mal necesario—
tenga otro idioma para nombrarlo:
como tengo también otro idioma
para nombrar aquel mundo, esa otra vida.

and its cool breath caressed me.
I was thirty-seven;
I was a grown man.
Now, a decade later,
I think of those young people and their poems
and I feel the pain and the nostalgia
they felt.

The tugboat was a large
ocher metal thing
that moved slowly
through the muddy waters of the Magdalena.
She carried drums of gasoline, Jeeps,
cattle, sacks of dried coconuts.
She was not a thing of beauty
but my family spoke
the word *remolcador*
—a tie between the town and the world beyond—
with an almost religious reverence.

It's curious that I have spent
a large part of my life
in river cities,
that one river turned into another
in my destiny,
although now, when I see
a tugboat plow the Hudson—
an ugly thing, a necessary evil—
I have a different language to give it a name,
as I also have a different language
to name that world, that other life.

BOGOTÁ

Regresaré y habrá cambiado
como cambian las cosas,
pero las calles que anduve,
mis casas en La Candelaria, en Palermo, estarán allí.
Los eucaliptos perfumarán sus lomas,
los colibríes desangrarán sus atardeceres,
las noches seguirán gélidas, neblinosas
y en la neblina pernoctarán mis fantasmas.

Ciudad donde amé como no he vuelto a hacerlo
ciudad que vive en mis sueños, como un ser
viviente con voz y aliento.
Regresaré a buscar un idilio desvanecido
tratando de rellenar mis huellas,
lo que conocí, y los cuerpos que amé
que ya no encenderán mi deseo.

Y en el futuro, mis historia se repetirá,
otro poeta partirá a perseguir sus sueños.
Así es esa ciudad, país donde quiero morir—
un dorado paraíso perdido
cementerio de mis deseos.

BOGOTÁ

I will go back and it will have changed
the way things change,
but the streets I walked,
my houses in La Calendaria, in Palermo, will be there.
The eucalyptus will perfume the hills,
hummingbirds will draw blood from the twilight sky,
the nights will be cold and misty,
and those mists will be peopled by my ghosts.

Bogotá, where I loved as I have not loved again,
Bogotá, that appears in my dreams like a living
being with voice and breath.
I will go back to look for a vanished idyll,
trying to fill the hollows in my soul,
the things I loved, the bodies I knew
but now will not inflame desire.

And in the future, my story will be repeated,
another poet will leave to follow his dreams.
That's how the city is, the landscape where I want to die
a golden lost paradise,
cemetery of my desires.

INVIERNO EN WALL STREET

La primera nevada ha caído.
La navidad será blanca
como este momento en el parque solitario—
un cementerio en desuso,
y corro en la nieve con los brazos extendidos
mientras pienso: Gracias al Señor Creador
de la nieve. Aleluya por este momento de luz,
por darme este instante,
por darle otra oportunidad a mi corazón y a mis ojos.

Todas las mañanas me levanto
para inspeccionar en el espejo
las arrugas en el rostro.
Me levanto en un cuarto vacío
con muchas ventanas por las cuales no entran
la luz ni los ruidos de afuera.
Y sin embargo, por qué siento este murmullo,
este sonido que se anida profundo en mi cerebro,
que nunca parte, llenando mi cabeza
como con una red tejida por Aracné—
este laberinto sin luz y de telarañas.

Sí, "de placeres y dulzores despojada"
está mi vida. Todo lo que tengo
en la noche es esta luz de luna
que se filtra a través de la cortina.
Entra un viento suave, como un soplo
o un arrullo, y la luna se desplaza
por su escalera de estrellas.

Sólo poseo esa luz nocturna—
blancuzca sobre el vientre—

WINTER ON WALL STREET

The first snow has fallen.
Christmas will be white
as it is this moment in the solitary park—
a deserted cemetery,
and I run in the snow, arms widespread,
thinking: All thanks to the Almighty Creator
of snow. Praise God for this moment of light,
for being given this instant,
for another blessing for my heart and eyes.

Every morning I get up
and look in the mirror to inspect
the wrinkles in my face.
I get up in an empty room
with many windows, though no light
or outside noises are coming in.
Why, nevertheless, do I hear this murmur,
this sound nestled deep in my brain,
always there, filling my head
like an intricate net woven by Arachne—
this lightless labyrinth thick with webs.

Yes, "devoid of pleasure and sweetness"
describes my life. All I have
in the night is this moonlight
filtering through the curtains.
A soft breeze blows in like a breath
of a dove's cooing, and the moon is climbing
its staircase of stars.

All I possess is this nocturnal light—
pale white upon my belly—

que acaricia la almohada sobre la cual
yazgo incapaz de conciliar el sueño.
Cuando salgo al día, ataviado
con mis atuendos de invierno,
me quedo traspasado por unos instantes
reconociendo la luz de hoy
siempre hablando un lenguaje diferente,
siempre extraña. En el Bowery los desamparados
se congregan alrededor de grandes hogueras,
calentando las manos, para pedir
la limosna de cada día. Sus manos están rojas,
cubiertas de parches verduzcos, de moho,
y los pies son muñones sin forma,
despellejándose, flores marchitas,
la piel abriéndose en pétalos
en un ceñido encaje. Este es el momento
en el cual vuelvo a dar gracias:
Gracias por el techo derruído y el pan duro,
por no ser uno de ellos.

El suelo permanecerá helado por muchos meses,
las calles serán trampas peligrosas.
Camino cuidadosamente
deslizándome sobre el hielo.
Mi corazón también está helado, y desespero
por saber si una vez llegado el deshielo...
Hay días en los cuales sólo creo en esto,
en los cuales desearía descansar para siempre,
un cuerpo helado en la nieve
totalmente rígido y alerta.

"La vía del tren subterráneo es peligrosa"
y tengo que aferrarme a las columnas.
Los cuerpos cercanos al tuyo
están fríos o cálidos, pero no importa,

that caresses the pillow where
I lie unable to fall asleep.
When I go out to meet the day, cloaked
in my winter clothes,
I stand transfixed for an instant
recognizing the new day's light
always speaking a different tongue,
always strange. In the Bowery the homeless
huddle around large bonfires
warming their hands and waiting
to be fed. Their hands are raw
and covered with greenish splotches
and their feet are shapeless stumps...
flayed... dying flowers,
skin peeling back into petals
within the tight bindings. This is the moment
when again I give thanks:
Thanks for my leaking roof and stale bread,
for not being one of them.

The ground will be frozen for many months,
the streets will be dangerous traps.
I walk with caution
skidding over the ice.
My heart, too, is frozen, and I despair
of knowing whether once the thaw has come...
There are days when I believe only in this,
days when I would like to rest forever,
an icy body in the snow,
rigid top to toe but alert.

"The subway track is very dangerous"
and I have to hold onto the columns.
The bodies nearest yours
are cold or warm; but that's irrelevant,

es la tristeza en los ojos,
son las miradas indiferentes o inquietas
las que te perturban y cada día,
lo reconozco, las lágrimas brotan
inagotables. Mis pensamientos están
helados, pero estoy vivo, o ¿por qué entonces
fluye desde mis adentros esta fuente cálida?

Wall Street es un valle sin salidas.
Me dejo arrastrar por la multitud,
busco la puerta que me dará la inyección de vida.
Gracias Señor por esta bendición,
porque tuyo es el dolor y el dólar y la computadora.

¿Cuántos días desde esa primera nevada?
Quemo incienso para la ofrenda,
respiro el humo de cada día.
Canto una canción, repito unas palabras
y me ajusto a mi dieta, a lo que he escogido,
a lo que la vida me ha donado.

Todo el día miro en la distancia
los barcos que pasan, los rompehielos.
Hay días en los cuales la nieve baja
en grandes trozos cubiertos de gaviotas impávidas.
Al mediodía cuando la luz es más fuerte,
a pesar del viento helado, salgo.
Battery Park está cubierto de nieve
y los árboles desnudos
despliegan sus cortezas amarillas.
¿Cuántos han orinado en sus troncos
lo orina roja de nuestra época?
Me recuesto contra las barandas,
miro al sol, buscando su calor
y si veo la luna sé

it's the sadness in the eyes,
it's the indifferent or troubled gazes
that disturb you, and that every day
I recognize, tears pouring
uncontrollably. My thoughts are
frozen, but I am alive, or else how
would that warm fountain be flowing from me?

Wall Street is a valley with no way out.
I let myself be pulled along with the crowd,
I look for the door that will be an injection of life.
Thank you, Lord, for this blessing,
because yours is the pain and the dollar and the computer.

How many days since that first snowfall?
I burn incense as an offering,
I breathe the smoke of every day,
I sing a song, I repeat a few words,
and I adjust to my diet, to the choices I have made,
to what life has given me.

All day I watch as ships pass by
in the distance, the icebreakers.
These are days when the snow comes down
in great chunks covered with fearless gulls.
At noon, when the light is strongest,
and despite the icy wind, I go outside.
Battery Park is blanketed with snow
and the naked trees
unfurl their yellow bark.
How many men have urinated against their trunks
the red urine of our epoch?
I lean against the railing,
I look toward the sun, seeking its warmth
and if I see the moon I know

que ésta es su estación inhóspita.
Si caminara sobre el hielo, deslizándome
¿cuántos pasos daría antes de que el hielo
se rompiera y me hundiera y me tragara?
¿Qué ve el que se ahoga debajo de una capa
de hielo? ¿Será posible que ya no quiera ver nada?
¿Hasta dónde arrastrará su cuerpo congelado el río?
¿Cómo organizarán la misión de rescate?

Las gaviotas y los patos
vuelan incesantes, buscando algo que comer.
Las palomas rebuscan entre los escombros,
los drogados se recuestan contra los árboles.
A veces la luz es fuerte y los edificios
se humanizan y al calentar un poco
los gorriones cantan y con ellos canta mi corazón.
¡Es justo que exista alguna alegría en mi vida!
Luego salgo del edificio, en fila, como una hormiga,
la luz del ocaso en los días claros
es como el reflejo del interior de una colmena.
Allá, en la otra orilla del río,
se levanta la Estatua de la Libertad,
en su mano una tea encendida
y encima de ella una estrella.
Cuando la multitud me empuja
hacia el subterráneo
pienso en los cielos, en templos a la luna.
Me siento agotado
pero estoy libre por unas horas
hasta que llegue el sueño.
Ahora conozco mis sueños:
tu rostro, con dos ojeras moradas,
flota enfrente de mis ojos.
A veces sueño que estoy dormido.
A veces sueño que estoy despierto.

that this is its desolate season.
If I walked out on the ice, slipping and sliding,
how far would I get before the ice
broke and I fell through and was swallowed up?
What does a drowning person see beneath a layer
of ice? Could it be that now he wants to see nothing?
How far would the river drag his frozen body?
How would they organize the recovery mission?

Gulls and ducks
are in constant motion, looking for scraps to eat.
Pigeons peck through the rubble,
drug addicts prop themselves against the trees.
Sometimes the light is strong and the buildings
take on human shape, and as they warm in the sun
the sparrows sing and my heart sings with them.
It's only fair that there be some joy in my life!
Then I leave the building, marching in line like an ant;
on clear days the light at sunset
is like the interior of an anthill.
There on the other bank of the river
stands the Statue of Liberty,
a lighted torch in her hand,
above her, a bright star.
As the throngs sweep me
toward the subway
I think of the heavens, of temples to the moon.
I feel exhausted
but I am free for a few hours,
until sleep finally comes.
Now I know my dreams:
your face, dark circles beneath your eyes,
floats before me.
Sometimes I dream I am asleep.
Sometimes I dream I am awake.

A veces, últimamente, sueño que no sueño.

Golpea mi corazón, oh Dios multifacético
Padre, Hijo y Espíritu Santo.
Porque ya no puedo soñar con los muertos,
descubro que he estado muerto todo este invierno.
Sé que después de aquí no hay allá
y escribo en mi diario: "Sin luz y a oscuras viviendo"
mis sueños cada vez más se parecen a la muerte.
Deseo habitar en un cuarto oscuro,
elaborado como un mausoleo,
propicio al sueño.
Tarde, todas las noches, el sádico
del apartamento vecino golpea y maltrata
a su perro, mientras grita:
"muere, muere, muere".
Y pienso entonces: ¿cómo pueden los vivos
ayudar a los muertos? ¿Quien sufre más:
el sádico, el perro o tú escuchándolos?
¿Y quien goza? Cuando tocas las flores
de Wall Street te electrocutas.

Un día de descanso le dio Dios al ser humano
y dos nos ha dado el capitalismo.
Sé que Dios nunca fue generoso
y que su hijo fue aún más tacaño.
Si yo pudiera multiplicar
el vino, el pan, los peces
abriría una fábrica de enlatados
en vez de ansiar ser crucificado.
Hay más de cien caídas al Calvario:
subway, tranvía, pastillas, drogas, sexo.

Bajo el ascensor repleto
y si la luz se fuera

Sometimes, lately, I dream I am not dreaming.

My heart pounds. O multifaceted God,
Father, Son, and Holy Ghost.
Because I can no longer dream of the dead
I discover that I have been dead all winter.
I know there is nothing beyond the here and now
and I write in my diary: "Living without light, in darkness."
My dreams are more and more like death.
I want to live my life in a room
dark as a mausoleum,
conducive to sleep.
Late every night the sadist
in the next apartment whips and kicks
his dog as he screams
"Die, die, die."
And then I think, how can the living
help the dead? Who suffers more,
the sadist, the dog, or the one listening?
And who gets pleasure? When you touch the flowers
on Wall Street you are electrocuted.

God gave man a day of rest
and capitalism has given us two.
I know that God was never generous
and that his son was even stingier.
If I could multiply
the wine, the loaves, the fish,
I would open a canning factory,
not crave crucifixion.
More than a hundred falls mark the path to Calvary:
subway, streetcar, pills, drugs, sex.

I take the crowded Down elevator
and if the lights were to go out

sería como una sala oscura,
un lugar para el sexo.
Los miro entrando en calor
mirando la película pornográfica
en la antesala, en la sala oscura,
antes de entrar. Adentro me esperan los sádicos,
los masoquistas, los masturbadores,
los solitarios, los carteristas, tu *doppelganger*,
el hombre de ahora, de este instante.

Escóndete, amanece, abandona
el recinto. No entregues tu ternura
en un cementerio de chatarra.
Así se repiten los días, las semanas, los meses
hasta que ni las nevadas,
ni el río, ni la luna, y a veces ni hasta la luz
ya no tienen significado.

¿Quién está vivo en este valle? grita
el loco, el profeta
el alucinado, el iluminado
el desechado, el escogido.
Gloria al Señor en las alturas, Aleluya,
el Juicio Final está a la vuelta de la esquina
estos edificios se derrumbarán
estas estructuras de hielo y de hierro
estos días de Sodoma y sodomía
y los justos serán llamados.
¿Quién es tu Dios? Él pregunta.
¿Quién es tu creador, a quién adoras?
Y tú te alejas del hombre
porque tú también tienes un mensaje:
Padre dólar que estás en el dólar
Santificado sea tu dólar
Vénganos a tu dólar y a tu menudo

it would be like a dark room,
a place to have sex.
I see them getting hot and bothered,
watching the pornographic film
in the lobby, in the dark room,
before they go in. Inside, sadists wait for me,
masochists, masturbators,
the lonely, the pickpockets: your doppleganger,
the man of today, of this instant.

Hide, wake up, flee
that place. Don't surrender your tenderness
in a junkyard.
And so the days, weeks, months, repeat and repeat
until not even the snowfall,
not the river, not the moon, sometimes not even light,
has meaning.

Who is alive in this valley? screams
the madman, the prophet,
the hallucinating, the illuminated,
the tossed aside, the chosen.
Glory to God in the highest. Hallelujah,
the Final Judgement is just around the corner,
these buildings will collapse,
these structures of ice and iron,
these days of Sodom and sodomy,
and the just will be called.
Who is your God? he asks.
Who is your creator, whom do you worship?
And you move away from that man
because you, too, have a message:
Our Father Dollar, which art in the dollar,
Blessed be thy dollar and thy small change
because within the dollar dwell pain

porque en el dólar reside el dolor
y tu reino.

Sabes que para ti no hay regreso.
Camina, anda, te esperan
cuarenta años en el desierto.
Da gracias, grita tus bendiciones
alégrate de no ser uno de ellos
da gracias al Señor Creador
de la nieve, de Wall Street
de lo que te has convertido.
Da gracias porque tú sabes que la venganza es eterna.
Salgan de sus sótanos zánganos y cobardes,
despójense de las máscaras y las pompas
rían, canten, celebren.
Yo sé mi oración y mi canción
y ella flota de mi boca:
Bendito sea el Señor y el Dólar
porque así es como termina el mundo
porque así es como termina el mundo
con un desquiciado gritando
mientras la nieve
cae y todos nos alejamos
Aleluya
Aleluya
Aleluya

1977

and thy kingdom.

You know that for you there is no return.
Go on, get started, they've been waiting for you
forty years in the desert.
Give thanks, shout your blessings,
be grateful you are not one of them,
give thanks to the Almighty Creator
of snow, of Wall Street,
of all that has converted you.
Give thanks because you know that vengeance is eternal.
Come out of your cellars, ye drones and cowards.
Cast off your masks and pageantry,
laugh, sing, celebrate.
I know my prayer and my song
and it floats from my lips:
Blessed be the Lord and the Dollar
because that is how the world ends
because that is how the world ends
with an unhinged man screaming
as the snow
falls and we all move away
Hallelujah
Hallelujah
Hallelujah

1977

LAS MUJERES

> Ella nos da su sangre, ella nos cría
> no ha hecho el cielo cosa más ingrata;
> es un ángel y a veces una harpía.
>
> *Félix Lope de Vega Carpio*

Cuando uno se despide ellas,
si están en su casa,
te ofrecen un envase de jugo de manzana,
una pechuga de pollo,
una rabanada de queso.
A diferencia de los hombres,
a quienes hay que pedirle las cosas,
las mujeres nos obsequian
almanaques, tarjetas, tortas.
Aprecian aún los gestos más insignificantes.
Si les obsequiamos flores perfumadas como las lilas,
o flores inodoras como las orquídeas,
o flores bellas, pero trilladas, como las rosas,
las mujeres se pavonean como gallinas cluecas
y se sienten amadas, Cleopatras, Marías Antonietas.
Sin las mujeres no existirían
los placeres burgueses:
ellas inventaron las almohadas,
las sábanas limpias y las recetas—
las feministas añadirían
que el cálculo y la trigonometría.
Hay artes enteras que no existirían sin ellas:
sin Lillian Gish, ni Marilyn, ni Garbo
el cine sería una cueva oscura.
Porque las mujeres—a menos que sean
primas de Emma Bovary—nunca
llevan sus hogares a la bancarrota
aunque las que rigen países o emporios

WOMEN

She gives us her blood, she cares for us as children,
heaven has not created a more thankless creature;
she is an angel, and sometimes a harpy.
Félix Lope de Vega Carpio

When you say goodbye, they,
if they are at home,
offer you a glass of apple juice,
a chicken breast,
a slice of cheese.
Unlike men,
from whom you have to request things,
women shower us with
almanacs, cards, and cakes.
They appreciate even the most meaningless gestures.
If we bring women fragrant flowers like lilacs,
or odorless flowers like orchids,
or beautiful if cliché flowers like roses,
they strut around like broody hens,
feeling they are loved: Cleopatras or Marie Antoinettes.
Without women we would have no
bourgeois pleasures:
women invented pillows,
clean sheets, and recipes—and feminists would add
calculus and trigonometry.
There are entire art forms that would not exist without them:
without Lillian Gish or Marilyn or Garbo
the cinema would be a dark cave.
Because women—unless they're
cousins of Emma Bovary—never
lead their households into bankruptcy,
though those who rule countries or empires
can make as big a blunder as any man.

meten las patas como cualquier hombre.
Porque las mujeres dicen
cosas como, "Te ves divina",
porque son chismosas
y se ríen entre ellas y con nosotros
y escuchan nuestras cuitas.
Porque practican el arte
de la amistad y se sacrifican
por toda clase de hombres idiotas;
porque son temibles si no les correspondemos
sus afectos; porque sin ellas
no existiría la poesía;
porque los primeros poemas
no fueron acerca de las estaciones
sino acerca de un pobre poeta
perdido por una de ellas.
Porque sin "Casta Diva" la ópera sería
aburridísima; porque son delicadas
y se perfuman y usan: pelucas
lentejuelas, zapatillas con tacón aguja,
vestidos justos y bikinis
y, sobre todo, porque se maquillan.
Porque sin ellas Adán tendría
todas sus costillas pero sería un onanista.
Porque son mitad diosas y mitad vacas;
porque una de ellas parió al hijo de Dios;
porque no hay mujer maluca.
Porque aún la más fea
es maternal y generosa.
Porque no son machistas
y si lo son, no tienen bolas.
Porque sin ellas no tendríamos
la Mona Lisa, ni los sonetos de Petrarca
ni La Divina Comedia.
¿Y qué sería de Romeo sin Julieta?

Because women say
things like "You look divine,"
because they're gossips
and laugh among themselves and with us
and listen to our troubles.
Because they practice the art
of friendship and sacrifice themselves
to all manner of idiotic men;
because they are fearsome if we don't match
their affections; because without them
there would be no poetry;
because the first poems weren't about the seasons
but about a poet
lost over one of them.
Because without "*Casta Diva*" the opera would be
deadly dull; because they are delicate
and smell of perfume and use wigs,
sequins, spike-heeled slippers,
tight-fitting dresses, and bikinis
and, most of all, because they wear make-up.
Because without them Adam would have
all his ribs but would be an onanist.
Because they are half goddesses and half cows;
because one of them gave birth to the son of God;
because no woman is without beauty.
Because even the ugliest among them
is maternal and generous.
Because they are not macho
but even if they are, they don't have balls.
Because without them we wouldn't have
the Mona Lisa, or Petrarch's sonnets
or *The Divine Comedy*.
And what would Romeo be without Juliet?
Don Quixote without his Dulcinea?
Don Juan and Casanova without the ladies?

¿De Don Quixote sin su Dulcinea?
¿De Don Juan y Casanova sin las doñas?
Porque aún si uno a veces las detesta
y usa "mujercita" como el peor insulto,
y no le interesan las mujeres para nada,
el mundo sin ellas sería
como la noche sin la luna
la tempestad sin las centellas.

Because if at times you detest them
and use the words "a real doll" as the worst insult,
and are not in the least interested in women,
a world without them would be
like the night without the moon,
the storm without the slash of lightning.

MI AUTOBIOGRAFÍA

Mi mayor ambición
es la de escribir al menos
un poema que sea leído en el futuro
por algún joven enardecido
quien exclame: " Manrique tenía cojones!"
Y este joven querrá haberse acostado
conmigo como yo me habría entregado
a Cavafis, Barba Jacob, Rimbaud, Melville
y sobre todo a Walt Whitman.
Y si llego a la vejez,
y me momifico en la piedad,
que nadie nunca olvide
que fui un borracho
un drogadicto
que por veinte años
vagabundeé por los continentes
me acosté
con miles de hombres
de todos los tamaños y colores
aunque mis favoritos fueron
los muchachos campesinos
y rubios de Nueva Inglaterra.
Y si es verdad
que vendí la sangre
el cuerpo
y hasta perdí mis ilusiones
nunca traicioné el don de mi poesía.

MY AUTOBIOGRAPHY

My greatest ambition
is to write at least
one poem that in the future will be read
by an inflamed youth
who will exclaim: "That Manrique had balls!"
And this same youth will wish he had gone to bed
with me, as I would have given myself
to Cavafis, Barba Jacob, Rimbaud, Melville
and, most of all, Walt Whitman.
And if I live to be an old man,
mummified in piety,
let no one ever forget
that I was a drunk
a drug addict
who for twenty years
wandered the continents
that I slept
with thousands of men
of all sizes and colors—
although my favorites were
the blond farm boys
of New England.
And if it is true
that I sold my blood
my body
and lost even my illusions
I never betrayed the gift of my poetry.

POESÍA

El misterio de la poesía
según Stephen Crane
consiste en que un hombre
puede dirigirse al universo
y el universo
le contesta.

POETRY

The mystery of poetry
according to Stephen Crane
is that a man can
address the universe
and the universe
will answer him.

PART TWO

TARZAN

Poems Without Translations

LEARNING ENGLISH, 1967

The summer I finished high school
Mother and I worked in the same factory
in Ybor City, the black section of town.

Mami sewed all day
in silence, she knew
only a few words in English.
I worked alone, sorting out huge containers
of soiled hospital linen
and I despised every moment of it.
I was eighteen; *Mami* nearly fifty.

After work, we took the bus home.
As the suffocating heat
lifted, and the mango tree
in our yard released fruity
scents and yielded shadow
the langorous stretch
before dark
was a time
to become human.

The apartment we lived in on Elmore Street
had linoleum floors
and termites in the furniture.
After our TV dinner
—we were so new in America these
dinners seemed another miracle of technology—
Mami visited Hortencia,
a Cuban refugee so overweight
she could not walk to our house
after a day of piecework.

We had no television, no telephone,
so I sat on the terrace
watched the elevated highway
next to the house and read
novels that transported me
far away from Ybor City.

On Saturday afternoons, I walked
to the old library in downtown Tampa
where I discovered, in Spanish,
Manuel Puig's *Betrayed by Rita Hayworth.*
I read this book at night
and during breaks at the factory:
a novel with a homosexual boy hero
that made me dream of glamorous
MGM technicolor musicals and goddesses
in slinky glittering gowns.
I was young.

Sitting on the porch
as dusk deepened
punctured by fireflies
darting stars weaving
in and out of the mangoes
I dreamt of distant cities
of leading a life
that had nothing to do with a factory,
not knowing
I would journey
away from Ybor City
exiled from the world of my mother
yet still be a survivor.

It's only now, when I think back
on the youth I was

that I can feel
heartache for my innocence
for my mother's silent fortitude
for our unspoken fears;
for lives that were hard
but rich in dreams.

IN OAXACA

I stood at the zenith
of the Pyramid of the Sun
at Monte Albán, and taking in
the emerald view,
I thought, there is no place
like this in the whole world,
a land where stationary clouds
hang like shrouds
made with feathers of mournful birds;
a land where death
is a woven cotton canopy
roofing the landscape.
And there are no people in the world
like the people who built this place,
and their descendants: children of a flaming flower
born under a sky of cochineal.

It is said that late in the afternoon,
after the tourists have gone,
the grasses of Monte Albán turn gold
to receive a mythic Bird of Paradise
that lands to seal up the passage
from light into radiant darkness with its song.

Summer nights, above the gardens of the *zócalo*,
a white moon—a livid mistress of the dead—
appears in a frosted sky.
She rises above the street lamps
lighting up the red Cannas and white roses
as an old man sings to
a group of youngsters in love
who sit at his feet.

He's their prophet, their minstrel, their troubador,
And he sings: "Because you're no longer by my side, dear heart,
I'm so wounded that I look for death."
Two enraptured young men join in:
"Ay lara lai, Ay lara lai."
The old man continues:
"With my guitar singing
I spend whole nights
under a mantle of stars."

In Oaxaca, the colors of life and death
are the same and its miracles are equally splendid;
and the air we breathe in is scented
with lyrics that make us listen
as they break our hearts.

PORTRAIT OF BOB GIARD

You've heard of Horace's
golden mean—the middle path?
...That's me. You could say
I'm a temperate kind of guy.
Everything in moderation.
I'm not slaphappy
but I'm content with my life.
I love what I do,
I may not have a lot of money
a lot of material things
yet, I live in a beautiful place
though I don't even own a car.
On sunny days, I bike down
to the beach for lunch.
Life doesn't get much better than that.
It's true I can't take much sun:
I tan very easily.
My father is French Catholic
and my mother Lithuanian...
people often think I'm of Scandinavian descent.
My father worked in a factory
where they made Royal typewriters,
it was across the street from our house,
the building just recently burned down.
In my opinion, what's really important in life
is to strike a balance.
Despite my Catholic upbringing—
I have an optimistic view of life.
I'm not a depressed person
I'm not on medication.
But then, I've been fairly lucky:
I've had two major relationships

and I'm still friends with my former lover.
My lover and I have been
together for over twenty years
and even though there have been rocky periods
we still love each other,
this summer we're gonna go biking in Holland.
I suppose if he ever left me
or I came down with a fatal illness
my outlook on life would change.
...We need to have an inner core
that nothing can touch
so that even when we are in pain and afflicted with sadness
we won't be derailed.
...I'm educated, I went to Yale
on a scholarship. And I 'm cultivated
and love refinement.
Not the kind of refinement that's really prissy
and repressed, the kind that doesn't
leave room for the randomness
and the messiness of life.
If I go into a place that's kind of bare
where everything is in a fixed place,
like in a museum
—if it looks rigid—
what I want to do
is to mess it up, to say,
"Hey, life's not like that, folks!"
...I guess I love to explain things
that's why I've taught most of my life.
To my students I say,
"I'm a fairly classical fellow
who's open to the spontaneous,
the unexpected,
that moment when
whatever we're inside

—the core of our beings, I spoke of—
shows through.
...I don't believe the camera's eye
can really capture character.
Some saintly people can look cruel...
monstrous people can look saintly;
sometimes I've caught
something prodigious, even sublime,
in a person
when the sitter was thinking
empty thoughts
or what they had for lunch.

GHOSTS AND THE LIVING

There was a time
when I didn't know
anyone who was dead—
let alone any ghosts.

But nowadays,
no longer confined
to the realm of night
or to lunar whiteness,
the ghosts seem to outnumber
the living.
Yet who's to say
they weren't always there
and I just wasn't
able to interpret
their colorlessness.

Tonight, above the pines near the house,
the full moon is the bleeding heart
of a cross of light.
She is herself a ghost,
a spectral diva,
wailing rivers of alabaster
for her subjects.

With the passage of time,
I've grown more adept
at reading the seemingly
empty spaces
of the universe;
I've learned that the void
teems with ghosts,

that the living are only ghosts
waiting to simplify;
that the still whiteness
of some nights
is nothing but a battalion of ghosts
weaving a tapestry like a tent
pinned to the ground,
that prevents traveling
to faraway
chilly galaxies.

Tonight the ghosts
are saying,
"Just because
we no longer seem
to be here
does not mean we
must be exiled to the tundra
of infinity.
We love hovering around this place,
content with being
the Northern Lights,
the halo around the moon,
the falling stars
of frosted skies.
Just because we speak
the language of light
does not mean we favor silence.
We'd like to speak through you,
so that our weightlessness
is not so misunderstood."

Lately, I'm more in touch
with ghosts
than with the living.

It's their language
I understand,
their every word I trust.
I understand their so-called
muteness
their cryptic signs
as clearly
as I understand, love,
your uneasiness
among the living.
That's why tonight
I ask you
to journey with me
through the platinum
of the moon's twilight.
When we talk
about the time we have left
on this earth
the years we have left
to love
produce
leave behind
our work,
it would be better
to remember someday
we'll, too, be ghosts
colonizing the vast spaces
of the universe;
that we'll whisper
invitations
to voyage
to the living
who miss us,
the way they seem to call tonight,
"Come with us, love...

for we, too, long for companions
for the clumsiness of flesh;
being all soul
we long for human decay
and are burdened, too,
with unanswered questions
wondering
if being ghosts is another
transitory state;
if we'll ever go back
to be one of you
so that we can feel again
the sweet torment of love."

Now that most of my loved ones
are ghosts; now that I
I spend more time in communion
with them than with the living,
I'm afraid to love, love.
I'm afraid
to surrender
to the flesh
the heart
the tyranny of light
demanding
we grow roots
in the realm of
the living.

BAUDELAIRE'S *Spleen*

All this fall
traveling on the Metro North
along the eastern shore
from Vermont to D.C.
the leaves
have been turning for months,
soon the trees
will be bare
their flushed leaves
covering the welcoming earth.

Today the train
passes by bronzed cornfields
and the rushing world
is a glowing canvas
that does not warm me.
An unshaved young man
sitting next to me
and writing in his notebook
awakens my curiosity.
He's like a matinee idol
of another era—
a young Leslie Howard.
When he's absorbed
contemplating the fiery landscape,
I glance at his notes:
"Finish reading the Baudelaire poem?"
he's written.
Which Baudelaire poem,
I wonder. And why the question mark?
Underneath this line he's added:
"Radio Shack—fractals."

My love,
since September
after a cold, pluvious summer
my days and nights
have been filled
with nostalgia for our future.
Neither you nor I
are like this youth
whose life just commences.
He has whole realms
to discover:
poems by Baudelaire
that will make him wonder
more than all the mysteries
of physics.
And he'll love—
if he hasn't loved yet—
and he'll suffer;
and if Fortune's kind to him,
he'll ride this train
on many occasions
until one day,
just like I do, at the end
of this autumn
of glad melancholia,
he, too, will travel
toward his loved one
toward arms and lips
that are an earthly home;
toward his future,
a continium of shared lives
until one day
he'll arrive
at an unknown—but familiar—place

like one of those Baudelaire poems
to which we return
years, lives
after having visited it
for the first time
when the future seemed limitless
and we could hold all our past
in a cupped hand.

To this youth
I say:
all this will pass
someday.
This autumn
our love
this city I travel to
this yearning for knowledge
and truth
these lines
will pass;
you and I
will pass
like the train passes
over these tracks
across these fields
of fallen leaves
and these blue skies
that remind me of your eyes
and all the icy-blue stars
that bloom at night;
and all my thoughts
great and small
and my dreams
and his and yours
they, too, will pass

until no one remembers them
except the memoriless earth
that feeds and replenishes
and prevails
after youth and love
and history
—and even Baudelaire's poems—
are no more.

INSCRIPTIONS FROM A LOST TABLET

A thousand horses wearing a thousand bells ride
the desert and begin the siege of our walled-in
city. The helmets of the invading warriors
gleam under the pitiless sun. The desert is a
chamber echo of sand. I am but one woman of my
Lord Tiglath-Pileser III. In our communal room
the women quiver with fear. I take solace fin-
gering my lapis-lazuli necklace. Already, my
wound is grievous. I know the cruelty of Assy-
rian soldiers: with their lances and arrows
they pierce the hearts of the conquered women,
and with whetted daggers they spear our hearts
to feed their lions. I know that after the
horses and the archers and the power of our Lord
have vanished, my necklace—pieced together and
re-strung—will tell my story to the world; it
will say more about me than a thousand tablets.
I pour oil from my alabaster jar to anoint each
bead of my necklace as I pray to Almighty Ishtar,
Goddess of War, but more important Goddess of Love.
I pray that my necklace—a concubine's keepsake—
will last so that I, who never conquered king-
doms or vanquished peoples, will prevail, and
though my story and my name will remain unknown,
the future will know of my love for the perfect
beauty of my gold and lapis-lazuli ornament.

POEM FOR MATTHEW SHEPARD

In the final moments
when the station wagon
pulled away, I shivered
and was thankful to feel something.
Blood glued my eyes.
I thought: the last thing
I want to remember
is not the look of hatred
in their eyes.
I breathed in the smell
of the grass that grew
before winter set in;
I heard the song
of nocturnal birds.
In my mind's eye
I saw shooting stars
the waning harvest moon
the light of dawn.
The wind swept over the plain
yanking the *matorral,*
a coyote howled,
perhaps a wolf,
a field mouse scurried
in the dark.
Later, I imagined
the birds lifting off
after the planets, rising
in the silvery skies.
As the warmth of day neared
I didn't dare hope
I'd be rescued.
Then my soul began

its upward ascent
a sigh traveling to
the arms of God
where I'd find
a peace I'd never known on earth.

1963

was the year
I started
getting up
at night
to play with my uncle
Giovanni's cock.
At night I'd watch him undress.
After he put out the light
I went to sleep
in a feverish state.
Waking up past
midnight
I'd skulk to his bed
pull out from his boxers
his cock
and hold it
in my shaking hand
until it would harden.
I didn't know what to do
with a cock—other than my own—
in my hands
so I held it in the dark
while the bats swooped
among the plantain trees
in our yard
while the night watchman
combed the streets
blowing his whistle
to say there were no prowlers
in the midnight
that the world was a safe place.
It was nineteen sixty-three

no cataclysms lit up the night skies.
As I held my uncle's cock
stroking it lovingly
placing it next to my cheek
breathing in
its pungent smell
I wondered whether Giovanni
—his body rigid
his chest heaving—
was asleep.
In the morning
I felt ashamed.
Giovanni never said
a word to me. He was
twenty-four years old
unemployed
with a lame foot
and he spent his days
reading the newspapers
waiting for his meals
while he drank sweet black coffee
and smoked *pielrojas.*
Each night
I waited for that moment
when desire would be so strong
I'd know no shame—
darkness protecting
my secret.
Then, one evening,
as I arrived home
from my English class,
Giovanni was sitting
on the porch reading a newpaper,
he looked up, and said to me:
"Marilyn's dead."

I hurried to our bedroom
threw my books and myself
on the bed, and wept.
That night, as I knelt
by Giovanni's side
I knew I'd go farther
than ever before.
I took his already hard cock
and put it in my mouth
and when I heard him sigh
the terror of that 13th year
of my life lifted
so that later
when the watchman blew his plaintive
whistle to announce
everything was fine
I felt peaceful
and unafraid
for the first time.

TARZAN

When I was thirteen
there was in my hometown
a man we called Tarzan
because of his build.
An outcast in Barranquilla
infamous for preying on youths
Tarzan's T-shirts
bandaged his torso;
he swaggered down the street
like a pied piper who could
drag behind him boys like me
and ruin us.

Late in the afternoons,
when the *amapolas* gashed
dusk with their scarlet
and the honeysuckle
infused the hour
with its sweet languor
Tarzan appeared
on my street
announced by the catcalls
of the neighbors
who, hiding behind their blinds,
called him names,
which he shook off
like a macaw, after preening,
shakes off its down.

Every afternoon I read
in a rocking chair
waiting for that moment
when he'd appear,

my heart beating so fast
I'd place an open palm on my mouth
as he strutted
a defiant animal
singing the song of perdition.
Not once did he ever look
in my direction
though he must have known I was there
because I felt the heat
of his ways—
a tongue of fire singeing me.

Tarzan's cat eyes bore
into my soul—
a bird with a burning beak
spearing the heart of a flower.
I was afraid Tarzan would expose me
for what I was—
someone like him, someone
who craved the touch of men.

Thirty years have passed
since that time.
I'm writing in a cabin in the woods
on top of a white hill.
It's been snowing all day
and I look out my window
through gleaming icycles.
Though Tarzan does not appear
now on my ghostly street
the longing I felt then grips me
reminding me of the pull of the flesh
bringing back memories
that still brand me
after all these years.

PART THREE

CHRISTOPHER COLUMBUS: REFLECTIONS ON HIS DEATHBED
(A COLLAGE)

CRISTÓBAL COLÓN: REFLEXIONES EN SU LECHO DE MUERTE
(UN ENCOLADO)

Translation by Edith Grossman
Introduction by Reinaldo Arenas

INTRODUCCIÓN

Las últimas alucinaciones, meditaciones, inquietudes y confesiones de Cristóbal Colón en su lecho de muerte integran el cuerpo de este poema de largo aliento, concebido y desarrollado con rigor y pulcritud verbal admirables.

Jaime Manrique asume la voz de El Almirante para realizar habilmente una instrospección y hasta una trasmutación sentimental a través del personaje histórico, desmitificándolo y convirtiéndolo en un individuo sufriente y mortal frente al esplendor incierto de la nada. Un ritmo sostenido y vibrante, una estructura perfecta, una vastísima erudición (que al autor tiene además la perspicacia de no hacerla evidente) concuerdan con el asunto desarrollado. Se intuye la voz del personaje poético—convertido en brillante metáfora de todas las pasiones—la sabiduría que tal vez otorgue la certeza de una muerte cercana.

El poeta logra traspasar la barrera de la crónica, del ditirambo y de la elegía circunstancial para entregarnos la vida imaginaria, desgarrada y contradictoria, llena de tinieblas y de fulgores, de una de las figuras más legendarias y polémicas de los tiempos modernos. La magia del poeta consiste en darle vida a documentos y papeles yertos, en hacer sangrar cartapacios polvorientos, en convertir el mito en hombre contrito, sufriente, ilusionado y desesperado que se confiesa ante nosotros con patética sinceridad de niño acorralado. La sabiduría de Jaime Manrique radica también en haber elaborado con el material histórico la materia de los sueños, poniendo la mano

INTRODUCTION

The final hallucinations, meditations, cavilations and con-
fessions of Christopher Columbus on his deathbed form the
substance of this wide-ranging poem, conceived and devel-
oped with admirable rigor and exactitude.

Jaime Manrique assumes the voice of The Admiral, artfully
creating introspection, even emotional transmutation in the
historical figure of Columbus. He is demythified and trans-
formed into a suffering mortal man confronting the uncertain
splendor of the void. Sustained, vibrant rhythm, perfect struc-
ture, and an immense erudition (the author possesses the wit
not to flaunt it) contribute to the poem's development. In the
voice of the poetic protagonist, who becomes a brilliant
metaphor for all the passions, we sense the wisdom that is
sometimes granted to us by the certainty of imminent death.

The poet goes beyond the limitations of the chronicle, the
dithyramb, the circumstancial elegy; he offers us the life of one
of the most legendary and controversial figures of the modern
age—an imaginary life that is heartbreaking, contradictory, full
of darkness and brilliant light. Magically, the poet animates
lifeless documents and papers, makes dusty archives bleed,
turns the myth into a contrite, suffering, hopeful, desperate
man who makes his confession with the pathetic sincerity of a
cornered child. Jaime Manrique has deftly interwoven the stuff
of dreams with the historical material by touching those tran-
scendent wounds.

en las llagas trascendentes.

Estamos ante una espléndida liturgia que es además un texto épico y subjetivo, alucinado y sosegado. Poema mayor, de esos que ya casi no se escriben, es a la vez un homenaje a las aventuras y a las tentaciones, ya sean espirituales o materiales, de una de las figuras centrales de nuestro caos latinoamericano.

Gracias a este poema el Quinto Centenario del "descubrimiento" de América contará con un texto decisivo (precisamente por su subjetividad o humanidad) para la interpretación del mismo. Resumen de angustias ciertas precisamente por parecer fantasmales.

Reinaldo Arenas
Nueva York, 1990

This is a spledid liturgy, a text that is epic, subjective, hallucinatory, and tranquil. A major poem, the kind of poem that almost no one writes anymore, it is a tribute to the adventures and temptations, both spiritual and material, of one of the central figures in the chaos of Latin America.

"Christopher Columbus on his Deathbed," with its subjectivity and its humanity, provides the Quincentenary of the "discovery" of America with a decisive text for the interpretation of that event—a tale of anguish that is true precisely because it seems phantasmal.

Reinaldo Arenas
New York, 1990

CRISTÓBAL COLÓN: REFLEXIONES EN SU LECHO DE MUERTE (UN ENCOLADO)

Mayo 29, 1506
Valladolid

Ahora que acepto mi muerte,
Mirando esta luz de mayo fuera de mi ventana,
Afable y dulce como un hálito divino
Que desciende acariciándonos, recuerdo
Las palabras del joven desconocido
De ojos brillantes quien
Como si acabara de descubrir un tesoro,
o ¿por qué no? de vislumbrar un nuevo mundo,
Me dijo: "Majestad, permítame besarle la mano
Al hombre más grande de nuestra era,
Al verdadero Emperador del Este".
Y yo, que tantos dominios he conquistado,
Como conquista al mundo esta luz de verano,
A medida que el sol se precipita
Hacia nosotros con su boca abierta,
Recuerdo esas palabras.
Porque ser Emperador implica
Haber conquistado otros mundos, abierto nuevas rutas,
Propagado el amor de Dios, llevado su bandera
E implantarla en el corazón de cada hombre.

        *   *   *

Me levanté de humildes orígenes,
Y mis hermanos no saborearon la gloria,
Excepto a través de mí.
Si me sentí el igual
De las Coronas de Castilla y Aragón
Fue porque siempre creí en el gran mensaje

CHRISTOPHER COLUMBUS: REFLECTIONS ON HIS DEATHBED (A COLLAGE)

29 May 1506
Valladolid

Now that I accept my death,
Looking through the window at May light
As gentle and sweet as the breath of God
Descending to caress us, I remember
The words of that young stranger,
His eyes shining, that boy, who
Said to me, as if he had just discovered
Treasure or—why not say it—glimpsed
A new world, "My Lord, allow me to kiss the hand
Of the greatest man of the age,
The true Emperor of the East."
And I, who have conquered countless domains
Just as the summer light conquers this world,
While the sun plunges toward us openmouthed,
Now I recall his words,
For Emperor suggests that I have conquered
Other worlds, opened other routes,
Carried the love of God, borne this banner
And planted it in the heart of every man.

  * * *

My roots were humble;
My brothers tasted no glory
Except through me.
And if I deemed myself the equal of
The sovereigns of Castille and Aragon
It was because I never lost my faith
In the great mission that was given me.

Que se me había encomendado.
Mi ambición fue monstruosa:
Exigí, antes de descubrir la ruta a Cipango,
Una décima parte de todos sus diamantes,
Perlas, metales, especias, frutas.
No sabía que también recibiría
Una décima parte de todas sus maldiciones
Y que más tarde me tildarían
De Descubridor de Mosquitolandía!

* * *

Está oscureciendo;
Pronto traerán una vela.
Más abajo, en fila india,
pero separada por vastos
Territorios no explorados,
dos estrellas se despiertan.
Ahora pienso: a los hombres se nos concede
Sólo un milagro en la vida.
Sé que la muerte se acerca en un coche alado
Y este momento, en el cual navego hacia la eternidad,
Es como el instante del descubrimiento.
Sé que en la otra orilla la Virgen me espera.

* * *

Las campanas de las diez me despiertan.
Han cerrado las ventanas.
Hay una lámpara encendida al pie de la cama.
No hay nadie en el cuarto. El médico descansa;
Mis hijos oran. Quisiera ver
Las estrellas precipitarse
Como una lluvia de fuego en el Atlántico.
Ahora sólo me falta escuchar el canto de los ruiseñores

My ambition was monstruous: I demanded,
Even before I discovered the route to Cathay,
A tenth part of all its diamonds,
Pearls, precious metals, spices, fruits.
How could I know I would also be granted
A tenth part of all its maledictions
Or that I would one day be called
Discoverer of Mosquitoland!

    *   *   *

It is growing dark;
Soon the candle will be brought.
A full moon rises.
Beneath it, in single file like Indians,
But separated
By vast unexplored territories,
Two stars awake.
I think of it now: we mortals are granted
No more than one miracle in our lives.
I know that death draws near in its winged chariot
And now, this instant, this voyage toward eternity,
Is like the moment of discovery.
I know the Blessed Virgin waits for me
On the other shore.

    *   *   *

The bells strike ten; I awake.
The windows are closed. A lamp
Burns at the foot of my bed.
The room is empty. The physician is resting;
My sons are praying. I should like to see
The stars hurtling down
Like a rain of fire over the Atlantic.

Oler el aire dulce de abril en Andalucía,
Sentir las olas mecer mi cama y oir por última vez el grito de
"Tierra!"...
Tierra...cielos alfombrados de papagayos,
Nativos de piernas fuertes y sin vientres,
Ninguno de ellos prieto, salvo del color de los canarios,
Del color del oro. Ese día escribí en mi diario:
"*Más me pareció que era gente pobre de todo....*"
Pobre de mí, que sólo sabía apreciar la riqueza por sus pompas,
Que desconocía la inocencia,
Y terminé devorado por su infierno.
Pobre de mí que pensé
Con cincuenta hombres podríamos sojuzgarlos.
Pero Cipango terminó apabullándonos,
El calor, el canibalismo, las fiebres nos dominaron.
La sífilis carcomió nuestros cerebros,
El paludismo nuestras vestiduras terrenales.
Como Moisés conduje mi gente a la Tierra Prometida,
Y una vez rota la promesa,
Terminamos esclavos de ella.

        *   *   *

No es verdad que fuí un mísero,
Que la avaricia me impulso a romper el dictum medieval:
"Allí donde está lo desconocido, imagínate los horrores."
Intercede por mí, Madre Redentora.
Apíadate de mí. Recuerdo que siempre, al anochecer,
Nos arrodillábamos sobre los maderos de la calabera
E invocábamos tus bendiciones.
Eia ergo, advocata nostra, illos tuos misericordes
Oculos nos converte. Et Jesum, benedictum fructum ventris tui,
Nobis post hoc exsilium ostende.
O clemens, o pia, o Maria.
El doctor entra al cuarto,

What I miss now is the song of nightingales,
The smell of sweet April air in Andalusia,
The feel of waves as they rock my bed;
I should like to hear for one last time
The sailor-shout of "Land!"
Land...skies blanketed with parrots,
Strong-legged, flat bellied natives
Not dark, canary-colored,
The color of gold. In my diary that day I wrote:
"They seemed, rather, a people woefully poor...."
Woe is me, knowing only the pomp of wealth
I was ignorant of innocence.
I came to save them
And I was the one devoured by their hell.
Woe is me, who thought just fifty of my men
Could vanquish them,
But we were the ones conquered by Cathay,
Crushed by its heat, its cannibals, its fevers.
Syphilis ate our brains away,
Malaria consumed our bodies.
Like Moses I led my people to the Promised Land,
A land that turned us into slaves
When the covenant was broken.

$*$ $*$ $*$

I was not a miser, it is not true
That avarice moved me to defy the ancient truth:
"Where the unknown is, there lies horror."
Intercede for me, Mary, Mother of us.
Have mercy on me. I remember that always
When night fell we fell to our knees
On the deck and invoked your blessing.
Eia ergo, advocata nostra, illos tuos misericordes
Oculus nos converte. Et Jesum, benedictum fructum ventris tui,

Sus ojos muy abiertos, aunque desde la puerta
No puede ver la expresión de mi rostro.
Cierro los ojos; finjo dormir,
Quiero estar a solas con mis recuerdos.

*   *   *

Ebrio de estellas descubrí la ruta hacia las Indias.
Por las noches, insomne, solitario,
En comunión con los astros,
Pensaba en mi fiel difunta esposa
Sin poder acompañarme en el momento del triunfo.
Pensaba también en Isabel la Católica,
Bendiciéndome desde su trono
Para que conquistase el amplio mar desconocido.
Y así, una noche, mientras escrutaba el cangrejo
Que un marinero había recogido,
Estudiando su caparaza para penetrar su misterio,
Pedro Gutiérrez se me acercó.
"Don Cristóbal", me dijo: "Este mar calmo y sin olas y sin viento
Nunca nos devolverá a España."
Sus ojos brillaban en la oscuridad
Como dos carbones de piedra;
Su piel, tostada y reseca por el sol,
Olía a sal, a mar abierto; y sus muslos
Hermosos por el trabajo intenso,
tenían cordilleras y sabanas
Que a mí me habría gustado explorar.
"Don Cristóbal", repitió,
"Entonces Ud. ha arriesgado su vida
Y la de sus compañeros, basándose en mera especulación".
"Así es", le dije; "no lo puedo negar.
Pero piensa en esto. Si ahora, tú y yo,
Y todos nuestros compañeros no estuviéramos
En medio del océano, en esta soledad desconocida,

Nobis post hoc exsilium ostende.
O clemens, o pia, o Maria.
The physician is entering the room now
Wide awake, though he cannot see
The expression on my face from the door.
I close my eyes and pretend to sleep,
I want to be alone with memory.

      *   *   *

Drunk with stars I discovered
The route to the Indies.
Traveling through the nights, sleepless and alone,
I communed with the stars and thought
Of my dear dead wife
Who could not share my triumph.
I thought of Isabel the Catholic,
Blessing me from her throne
That I might conquer the wide and unknown sea.
One night as I studied a crab
Caught by a sailor,
Searching the mystery in its shell,
Pedro Gutiérrez came to me.
"Don Christopher," he said: "This calm sea,
This waveless, windless sea
Will never take us back again to Spain."
In the darkness his black eyes
Shone like coals;
His skin, brown and dry with the sun,
Smelled of salt, of open sea, and his thighs
Made beautiful by labor
Had mountains and savannas
I would have liked to explore.
"Don Christopher," he said again,
"Then you have risked your life

En un estado de incertidumbre y peligro,
Si así te parece, ¿en qué otra forma
Pasaríamos nuestras vidas?
¿Quizá más contentos? ¿O acaso no estaríamos
En aprietos más grandes, o más solos,
O tal vez agobiados por el tedio?
No trataré de convencerte con la gloria
Que llevaremos de regreso, si esta aventura culmina bien
Como lo espero. Pero si de esta navegación no ganáramos más,
Me parece provechosa porque nos libra del aburrimiento,
Nos hace ver cuán rica y valiosa es la vida,
Le da valor a muchas cosas que de otra forma
Pasarían inadvertidas".

       *   *   *

No siempre fui un hombre justo.
Si he de reunirme con los que amo y he amado,
Tengo que pedir perdón por mi ambición y crueldad.
Rodrigo Bermejo, pide permiso y sal
Del océano de los muertos; háblame.
Te robé los diez mil maravedíes que te correspondían
Por ser el primero en avisar tierra.
Y por mi avaricia, tú, al regresar al viejo mundo,
Amargado y sin Fe, emigraste al Africa
Y te convertiste en Moro....
¿De qué nos servía cantar todas las noches:
Salve Regina Mater Misericordiae
Si mi corazón estaba podrido?
Por eso el Señor decretó un diluvio
Una vez llegados a las Indias.
Por eso la luna de tres cuartos
Que nos recibó al final del viaje
Cambió dos veces, en la oscuridad, en la lluvia
Antes de reaparecer.

And the lives of your comrades
For a mere guess."
"Yes," I said, "that I cannot deny.
But think of this. If you and I
And all our comrades were not
In the middle of the ocean,
In this unknown solitude,
In danger and uncertainty, just as you say,
Then what else would we do
With our lives?
Would we be happier? Or perhaps
At greater risk, or more alone,
Or even suffering from tedium?
I will not try to sway you with the glory
We will bring back with us, if this adventure
Goes well, as I desire.
But if we gain nothing else
This voyage seems worthwhile to me,
For it frees us from ennui,
It makes us see
How desirable life is, how rich,
How valuable the multitude of things
We would let pass unnoticed."

*   *   *

I have not always been a decent man.
If I am to meet again with those I love,
And have loved, then I must beg forgiveness
For ambition and cruelty.
Rodrigo Bermejo, ask leave to rise up
From the ocean of the dead and speak to me.
I stole the ten thousand maravedis
That rightfully were yours because you were
The first to sight land. And because

No quiero delirar! Quiero recordar bien las cosas;
Quiero poner orden antes del fin.
No quiero confundir los hechos
Ni olvidar nada.

    *   *   *

Las campanas de las doce suenan.
El doctor está roncando en una silla
Al lado de mi cama. Esta es la hora
De los fantasmas. Los rostros del pasado
Se desprenden de las tinieblas para llegar a mí.
Guacanagary; las tres sirenas que, en un viaje
De exploración, emergieron de las aguas del río.
Me imagino a los habitantes de la isla de Aván
(Isla que jamás visité), seres
Humanos con colas de animales,
Y esas bestias prehistóricas, las iguanas,
Capaces de cambiar no sólo de piel, sino de entrañas.
Obviamente no había llegado a Cipango,
Pues estas islas eran sólo un lugar
Que el Gran Khan utilizaba para abastecerse de esclavos.
Y si es verdad que mis discípulos eran piratas,
Convictos escapados, ladrones, asesinos, asaltantes,
Falsificadores y maleantes del Reino,
Cómo podía entregarle a Guacanagary
La carta de vuestras Majestades:
"*Fernando e Isabela al Rey de X*
Los soberanos se *han enterado de que el Rey de X*
Y sus súbditos aman a los Reyes de España.
Es más, están informados de que él
Y sus súbditos están ansiosos de tener noticias de España.
A este efecto han enviado a su Almirante Cristóbal Colón,
Quien les dará noticias suyas y les dirá que los Reyes se encuentran
Gozando de salud y en perfecta prosperidad".

Of my greed you returned to the Old World
Bitter, faith lost, and you left
For Africa to become a Moor....
To what avail the nightly singing
Salve Regina Mater Misericordiae
If my heart was rotting to the core?
That is why God sent us a deluge
When we finally reached the Indies.
That is why the three-quarter moon
Welcoming us at the end of the voyage
Had to come round twice, in darkness, in rain,
Before we could see it again.
I do not want delirium! I want to remember
Things as they were; I want
To put things in order before the end.
I do not want to confuse the facts,
I do not want to forget a thing.

       *   *   *

The bells strike twelve.
The physician is snoring in a chair
Beside my bed. This is the hour of phantoms.
Now I can see the faces from the past
Rising out of the shadows, approaching me.
Guacanagary; as we sailed the river
Three sirens rose up from its waters.
And I can see the folk of Aván Isle
(An island I never visited)
Humans with the tails of animals,
And iguanas, those prehistoric beasts
That could shed not only their skins
But their innards too.
It was clear I had not come to Cathay,
Clear these islands were no more than where

Marco Polo simplemente
No conoció los extremos de las Indias,
Sus puntos de abastecimiento.
Fue fácil concluir que éstos eran seres inferiores,
Y por eso, cuando encalló la Santa María
Disparé cañonazos desde la Niña
Y destruí lo que quedaba de la carabela
Para demostrarle a los nativos el poderío de España,
La rabia y el fuego que descenderían del cielo
Si no respetaban a los Dioses Blancos.

Cinco meses después, de vuelta al viejo mundo,
Los fariseos no tardaron en criticarme:
Había perdido la Santa María en el viaje
Y quizá, también, La Pinta.
Había abandonado a súbditos españoles
En un territorio desconocido
Que no volvería a encontrar.
¿Y dónde estaban las riquezas de que hablaba
Marco Polo? ¿Dónde estaba el oro?
Pero para la Reina el descubrimiento
Era más importante que los tesoros.
Así, en Barcelona, por primera vez conocí
Días felices, libres de ansiedad y desasosiego.
Meses más tarde decidí regresar,
Porque no había encontrado el Catay civilizado
Sino su antesala. Y luego, en el segundo viaje, descubrí:
No el oro, sino los cuerpos masacrados de los hombres
Que se habían quedado por orden mía;
Que los perros mudos y extraños

The Great Khan supplied himself with slaves.
And if it is true that my followers were
Pirates, thieves and forgers, escaped
Convicts, all the kingdom's thugs and killers,
How could I give to Guacanagary
The letter from Their Majesties:
"*The Sovereigns have learned that the King of X*
And all his subjects love the Crowns of Spain.
Moreover, they have been informed
That he and his loyal subjects long to know
The news from Spain.
And therefore they have sent their Admiral Royal,
Christopher Columbus, to convey to you
The news that their Royal Majesties
Enjoy good health, perfect prosperity."

    *   *   *

Marco Polo simply never knew the far
Ends of the Indies, the outposts.
How easy to assume such creatures as these
Were inferior. And therefore
When the Santa María ran aground
I ordered the Niña's cannons to turn on her
And I destroyed what remained of the caravelle
To prove to the natives the power of Spain,
The fury, the fire that would rain down from heaven
If they failed in respect for the White-skinned Gods.

    *   *   *

Five months later I returned to the Old World
To face the Pharisees attacking me:
I had lost the Santa María on that voyage
And perhaps the Pinta as well. And I had

Eran utilizados como alimentos,
Y que la principal función de las esclavas
Era parir niños gordos, color de manzana,
Para ser asados como cerdos.

*　　*　　*

El oro no fue mi principal ambición,
Aunque el oro buscaba.
Porque si no se encontraban las riquezas
Materiales en Cipango,
¿Dónde había aire más dulce, árboles más vistosos,
Frutas más sensuales, pájaros más exóticos?
¿Costas tan verdes y coloridas que no sabía
Adónde dirigirme primero? Del alba
Al crepúsculo, los ojos no se cansaban de observar
Esa vegetación tan diferente a la nuestra.
El perfume de las flores eran tan fuerte
Que inflaba las velas de las carabelas.
En este viaje empecé a capturar
Los indígenas para enviarlos a España.
No para esclavizarlos,
Como se me ha calumniado,
Sino para convertirlos a la verdera Fe,
Para enseñarles nuestra lengua
Y así pudieran regresar a sus islas
Para propagar la doctrina de Cristo.
Es verdad que como Virrey fui duro:
Que decapité, mutilé, quemé en la hoguera,
Y descuarticé a los rebeldes.
Pero el calor, las visiones, los mares blancos,
Espectrales, aterradores, lechosos,
Empezaron a carcomer mi mente, empezaron
A confundir la elusiva realidad con la fantasía.
No pido perdón por los seres cuyas vidas

Abandoned Spanish subjects in unknown lands
That I would never find again.
And where were the riches that Marco Polo
Described, the treasure of gold? But the Queen
Was moved by discovery, not treasure.
And so in Barcelona, for the first time
I knew contentment, days free of unrest
And tribulation. Months later
I decided to return, for what I'd found
Was not high old Cathay but its antechamber.
And then, on the second voyage, I discovered
Not gold, but the massacred bodies
Of men I had ordered to stay behind;
I discovered that the strange, mute dogs
Were used as food; that the principal labor
Of female slaves was to produce plump apple-
Colored babies that were roasted like suckling pigs.

      *   *   *

Gold was not the heart of my ambition
Although I did seek gold. But if I did not find
Treasure in Cathay, where in the world was the air
Sweeter, the trees more beautiful, their fruits
More sensual, the birds more extravagant?
Coasts so green, so high-colored I never knew
Which one to sail to first. From dawn to dusk
My eyes never wearied of observing
That vegetation so different from our own.
The scent of the flowers was so intense
It filled the sails of the caravelles.
On this voyage I began to capture natives
To send them back to Spain. Not, as my false
Accusers claim, to make them slaves,
But to convert them to the one True Faith,

Tronché o destruí; todo lo hice por la gloria de España.
Pues el oro lo quería para marchar a Jerusalem
Y liberarla de los infieles.
La gloria no para mí, sino para la Cristiandad
Y para mis descendientes.
¿Quién en un mundo sin leyes,
En un infierno que nos carcome,
Puede medir sus poderes exactos
Y seguir los razonamientos
De nuestro vano y vulnerable corazón?

      *   *   *

Desde el principio intuí como terminaría
Esta aventura, aunque nunca me imaginé
Que después del tercer viaje, volvería a España encadenado.
Cadenas que he cargado conmigo siempre
Y que ahora, mientras muero,
Reposan al pie de mi cama.
Durante ese viaje nos encontramos
Con los vientos muertos, y nueve días después de abandonar
Las Islas de Cabo Verde el calor se volvió agobiante.
Los rumores que habíamos oído de ser quemados
Vivos parecían ser verdad. Fue en ese instante que yo,
El gran descubridor, empecé a odiar los descubrimientos.
En las noches, mis ojos enfermos
Ni siquiera podían consolarme las estrellas.
Poco a poco el viento volvió a soplar.
Una mañana con un cielo reposado, de nubes claras,
Avistamos la Costa de Paria. Entonces
Sentí que nos acercábamos no a Cipango
Ni a Catay, sino al Paraíso del Viejo Testamento.
Ese día escribí en mi diario:
"No creo que sea una montaña elevada.
La tierra se eleva gradualmente, comenzando

To teach them our Spanish tongue
That they might return to their pagan isles
As missionaries of Christ's Holy Doctrine.
I do not deny my harshness as Viceroy:
Rebels were decapitated, mutilated,
Drawn and quartered, burned at the stake.
But the heat and its visions, the terror of seas
Turned milky white and ghostly, began to gnaw
At my mind, began to confuse elusive
Reality with fantasy.
I do not repent of the lives I shattered,
The creatures I killed;
I did it all for the glory of Spain
Hungry for gold to pay for its crusade
To free Jerusalem from the Infidel.
The glory was not for me, it was glory
For all of Christendom, for my descendants.
In a world that knew no law, in that hell
Of rot and decay,
Who could recall the limits of power
Or heed a vain and vulnerable heart?

*   *   *

From the beginning I knew how this
High adventure would end, though I never dreamed
That after my third voyage I'd be sent
Back to Spain in chains, these chains I've
Carried with me ever since. Now that I am dying
They rest there, at the foot of my deathbed.
During that voyage the wind died; we were becalmed,
And nine days after we sailed away
From the Cape Verde Islands
The heat overcame us.
Rumors we'd heard of being burned alive

En regiones lejos de aquí. El Paraíso
Está situado en un lugar al cual nadie puede llegar
A menos que sea con la intervención DIVINA.
Tiene la forma del pico de una montaña,
Que se parece a la parte inferior de una pera:
Una bola coronada con una protuberancia,
Como el pezón de un pecho femenino,
La tierra se hincha a través suyo
Y se acerca al cielo. Estas son las indicaciones
De que hemos llegado a la Vida Eterna".

   * * *

No habíamos llegado al Paraíso.
El Paraíso siempre estaría más allá.
Y sólo ahora, mientras muero, me siento
Cercano a sus puertas, a su umbral sin límites.
En ese instante debí haber obligado a mis hombres
A firmar una declaración para atestiguar
Que habíamos cruzado, no el mar, sino el espacio infinito.
Cómo explicarnos de otro modo
Las maravillas de estas tierras extrañas:
Millares de tortugas conformando islas
Donde las carabelas podían anclar;
Tempestades de mariposas como confetti viviente,
Corvejones con crestas de arcoiris dobles,
Conchas llenas de carnes, deliciosas
como manjares de dioses,
Y ostras hermosas, de mil colores, pero sin perlas....
Dos años y nueve meses navegando,
Y el continente que en un principio
Había parecido el Paraíso,
Ahora se trasformaba en un infierno:
Los marineros desesperados, sexualmente hambrientos;
Coanabo, a quien quería trasladar a España

Seemed to come true. That was the moment when
I, the great discoverer, despised discoveries.
At night my aching, ailing eyes
Could find no consolation in the stars.
Then slowly the wind rose once more. One morning
Under a tranquil sky, a few bright clouds,
We sighted the Coast of Paria. And then
I felt we were approaching not Cathay,
Not the Empire of the east and the Great Khan,
But Eden, Scripture's Earthly Paradise.
That day in my diary I wrote:
I do not believe it to be a mere mountain.
The land makes a gradual ascent, starting
Its rise in the distance. Paradise is
A place no man can reach unless he has
God's blessing. Its mountain shape
Resembles the lower portion of a pear:
A round form crowned by another, smaller form.
The land swells like a woman's breast, the nipple
Reaching toward heaven. These are the signs
That we at last have found Eternal Life.

*   *   *

No, we had not come to Paradise,
Paradise would forever lie beyond.
And only now, near death, can I draw near
Its infinite portal. But that was when
I should have forced my men to sign in witness
That we had crossed not Ocean but endless space.
How else explain the marvels of those strange lands:
Thousands of tortoises willing to act as islands,
Accepting the anchors of the carvelles;
Tempests of butterflies like living confetti,
Cormorants crested with double rows of rainbow,

Para que regresara a contar sus maravillas,
Muerto en el viaje. Dos años y nueve meses de sufrimiento,
De castigo por mi inconmensurable orgullo.
Entonces, vestido con el pobre hábito de un Franciscano,
Decidí practicar las tres virtudes esenciales:
Pobreza, Castidad, Obediencia.
Pobreza de imaginación, porque me sentía vencido,
Y mis muchos cofres vacíos, llenos de telerañas;
Castidad, al ver a los marinos copular
Desenfrenadamente a la luz de la luna
Y hacerme avances obscenos;
Obediencia a los nobles de España
Que venían a poner en su sitio al extranjero
Descubridor de un mundo que se convertía
En el cementerio de los Hidalgos castellanos.
Así, encadenado como un caballo,
Hice mi viaje de regreso en el vientre del barco.
Más nunca fui prisionero,
Excepto de mis sueños, mis pesadillas.
La única prisión que conocí fue la tierra,
Nunca el mar desconocido. Entonces
Recorrí los pueblos de España encadenado,
Cargando jaulas repletas de loros y pagagayos,
Y precedido en mi viacrucis de pueblo en pueblo,
Por indios adornados con plumas celestiales y objetos de oro.
Si no encontramos a Cipango con sus riquezas
Tal esplendor era desconocido al mundo,
Mensajeros tan deslumbrantes jamás habían aparecido.
La vieja nobleza triunfó,
Pero moralmente salí victorioso.
Así me lo hicieron ver mis gentes de España
Al verme humillado. Así me lo hizo ver mi amada
Reina, a cuyos pies me postré
Desconsolado, y quien con voz trémula
Y entre lágrimas me dijo:

Shellfish as sweet as the nectar of the gods,
Gorgeous high-colored oysters that had no pearls....
Two years nine months we sailed, and the continent
That first seemed Paradise was now transformed
Into an inferno: the sailors despaired,
Hungering for sex; I asked Coanabo to return
To Spain to recount the marvels we had seen.
Coanabo died on the way. Two years
Nine months of suffering, of punishment
For my overweening, immeasurable pride.
Then I donned the penitential habit
Of a Franciscan, vowed devotion to
The three essential virtues: Poverty,
Chastity, Obedience would be mine.
Poverty of imagination:
I had been vanquished, my many coffers
Were empty, filled with cobwebs;
Chastity after I saw the sailors
Copulate unrestrained in the moonlight
And dare make their obscene advances
Even to me;
Obedience to the noblemen of Spain
Who came to see the shaming of the foreigner,
Discoverer of a world that had become
The graveyard of Castillian Nobility.
And chained like an untamed horse
I voyaged home in the belly of a ship.
Never again was I made prisoner
Except of my dreams, my nightmares.
Land was the only prison I had known,
Never the uncharted sea.
In chains I traveled the cities of Spain,
The hamlets, bearing cages of parrots
And macaws; on this my *via crucis*
From town to village, village to town

"Levántate, mi Gran Almirante,
Portador de Cristo a través del océano.
Levántate y mírame a los ojos,
Porque tú, que tantas maravillas has visto,
Ya no eres mortal, sino Ulises divino....".
Así los culpables fueron castigados,
Yo y mi nombre y el de mis hijos reivindicados,
Y por eso me lancé al cuarto y último viaje.

      *   *   *

Cómo desearía levantarme de mi cama
Y contemplar la estrella polar.
El alba debe estar cerca,
Afuera escucho voces:
Alcanzo a reconocer las de Fernando y Diego.
Si tan sólo hoy pudiera salvarme
Como me salvé de morir de hambre en el cuarto viaje.
Pero en mi copia de Regiomantanus
Sólo se encuentran anunciados los eclipses, no las muertes.
¿Será la muerte realmente negra?
¿Tendrá su mensajero un rostro?
¿Seré capaz de reconocerlo llegado la hora?
El 29 de febrero de 1504,
Con mis barbas y cabello canos al viento
Le anuncié a los caníbales y paganos Caribes
Que la luna moriría sino nos proporcionaban alimentos.
Cuando empezó el eclipse entré a mi cabina.
Podía oir las imploraciones de la tribu
Para que detuviera la agonía del astro selenita.
Marqué el tiempo con mi reloj,
Y un poco antes de que terminara el eclipse
Salí a la proa y les anuncié que habían sido perdonados.
¿Cuántas clases de perdones podemos conceder,
Y cuántas se nos otorgan?

Indians adorned with gorgeous feathers
And rich gold walked before me. We did not find
Cathay with all its treasure, yet the world
Had never seen such splendor,
Such dazzling messengers.
The nobles of ancient lineage triumphed,
But moral victory was mine. Or so said
My partisans in Spain when I was humbled.
My beloved Queen made me see it clear
When I threw myself at her feet, disconsolate,
And she with tremulous voice, tears in her eyes
Said: "Arise, Great Admiral, my Standardbearer
Of Christ across the Ocean Sea. Arise
And look at me with eyes that have beheld
So many wonders you are now divine
Ulysses, no mere mortal..."
The culpable were punished and I, my name,
My children's name restored by law; therefore
I set out on my fourth and final voyage.

2

How I wish I could rise up from bed
And behold the Polar Star.
Dawn must be near. Outside I hear voices:
I recognize those of my sons.
Oh Fernando, Diego, if only today
I could be saved as we were saved
On that fourth voyage from starvation.
But my copy of Regiomantanus
Foretells eclipses, not deaths.
Is death really black?
Does her messenger have a face?
Will I recognize him when my hour comes?
On the twenty-ninth of February,

Tal vez reconocerlas sea
La única señal de muerte.
Pido perdón a Dios por mi arrogancia;
A mis hijos por el calor que no les di,
Por la palabra amable que nunca supe prodigarles,
Ni el contacto de mis manos sobre sus cabezas—
Los tiernos gestos cotidianos.

      *   *   *

Conocí un sólo tema,
Pues siempre estuve pasmado
Ante el sublime espectáculo del océano.
Y si no fui buen padre, ni estadista,
Como acto de contricción no podría pedir perdón
Por mis descubrimientos.
¿Qué significan esas luces filtrándose por las ventanas?
¿Ha escuchado la luna mi plegaria
Y se acerca una vez más para consolarme?
Protégeme luz divina,
Reconfórtame en esta hora aciaga,
Resguárdame de mis culpas, de las heridas auto inflingidas....
¿Estaré delirando? No, es la Reina.
Escucho su voz, como escuché
La voz de Dios en el cuarto viaje:
"No temas y ten confianza.
Todas estas tribulaciones
Están escritas en tablas de mármol
Y no por simple arbitrariedad mía".
Perdóname Isabel por no conseguir el oro prometido;
Por convertirte en mercader de esclavos;
Por ultrajar tu nombre y el de Castilla;
Por sembrar el odio en el corazón de los indígenas.
¿Quién nació, excepto Job,
Que no muriera desesperado?

In the year of Our Lord 1504,
My gray beard and hair blowing in the wind,
I announced to the Caribe Indians,
Caribe Cannibals, Caribe Pagans
That the moon would die unless they gave us food.
When the eclipse began I turned and walked
Into my cabin. There I could hear
The tribe imploring me to bring to a halt
The death agony of Selena's star.
I measured the time with my hour glass,
And just before the eclipse was to end
I walked out to the prow and told them
They had been forgiven. How much forgiveness
Can we grant, how much is granted us?
Perhaps knowing that is our one sure sign of death.
May God forgive me for my arrogance,
My sons for the warmth I never gave them,
The loving words I failed to say,
The ordinary acts of tenderness.

      *   *   *

One idea and one alone could move me;
Always the sublime sight of the ocean
Overwhelmed me. I never was a good father,
A good statesman, but in no act of contritrion
Could I beg that my discoveries be forgiven.
What light is this filtering through the windows?
Has the moon heard my prayer and come again
To bring me consolation? Heavenly light
Protect me, comfort me in this my fateful hour,
Shelter me from my sins, from the wounds I've inflicted...
Am I delirious? No, it is the Queen!
I hear her voice as once I heard
The voice of God on the final voyage:

Tú llegas ahora para facilitarme
El camino hacia las tinieblas.
Muero seguro de haber cumplido mi misión,
De haber ensanchado el mundo, lo que Dios creó,
Para provecho y bienestar de los hombres.
Isabel, no pidas perdón por olvidarme
En tus últimos deseos
Pues te acordaste de tus vasallos indios,
Lo cual equivale a acordarse de mí....
Yo, que tantas historias te conté para aliviar
Tu apesadumbrado corazón,
Cuéntame ahora de tu presente morada.
¿Es la nueva vida libre de espejismos?
¿O existen lluvias interminables
Como las de Cipango? Lluvias de sesenta días.
Pensé que perdería las carabelas
Y los hombres que me habías encomendado.
No sé si hombre alguno ha sufrido tal martirio!
La luz se va...Isabel, regresa y respóndeme.
Mis ojos nublados, ciegos no puden distinguir nada.
¿Qué es esta mancha negra y llena de voces acercándose?
Algo agarra mi mano fría y sudorosa.
No quiero morir todavía;
Quiero volver a ver la luz del día,
Experimentar una última aurora.

     *   *   *

Esa luz calcinante, resplandeciente,
Es como el mar de fuego
Que encontramos en el cuarto viaje.
Ese fuego que nos rodeaba
Inflando nubes de vapor
Soplando olas enloquecidas por el viento.
O como el mar de sangre,

"Do not be afraid. Have faith. These
Tribulations are inscribed in marble;
They are not the children simply of my whim."
Isabel, forgive me for never finding
The gold I promised you, for turning you
Into a trafficker in slaves, for offending
Your name and the name of all Castille, for sowing
Seeds of hatred in the Indians' hearts.
What man except Job was not born to die in despair?
You come now to ease my journey into darkness.
And I can die, certain I fulfilled my mission,
That I enlarged the world God had created
For the benefit of man. Isabel,
Do not ask my forgiveness: you forgot me
In your will, but you remembered your Indian
Vassals, which means you remembered me...
I who recounted endless tales to ease
The burden of your heavy, grieving heart,
I ask you now to tell of your resting place.
In the next life are we free at last of illusions
Or are there eternal downpours like the
Cathay rains that lasted sixty days? I thought
I'd lose the carvelles and all the men
You commended to my care. I do not know
If any other man has ever suffered
A martyrdom like mine! The light is fading...
Isabel, come back and answer me.
My clouded eyes see nothing...
What is this darkness, dark and full of voices,
That draws near? This something clutching at
My cold perspiring hand? Don't let me die,
Not yet, I want to see again the light
Of day, just one last dawn.

       *   *   *

De aguas rojas, un caldero
Sobre un fuego satánico.
¿Era la sangre real o una ilusión óptica?
¿O era esa la sangre de los indígenas
Que se suicidaban colgándose o envenándose,
Y que luego tirábamos al mar
Donde eran despedazados por las bestias marinas?
Entonces empecé a renegar de Dios:
La malaria, fiebres, enfermedades
Habían carcomido mi cerebro y los de los marineros.
Si no construímos un ídolo fue
Porque no encontramos el oro
Aunque estaba allí
Detrás de las islas encantadas
Que tejían un laberinto
Alrededor de Caty y sus dominios.

*   *   *

Repican las campanas.
Una, dos...son cinco, se acerca el día.
Escucho el fragor de las olas
Contra los acantilados.
Catay...El Gran Khan...el oro...los suicidas....
Así navegamos extraviados, penetrando mares
Cada vez más densos y peligrosos.
Finalmente llegamos a una costa
Cubierta de árboles frutales,
De ríos de aguas cristalinas,
Del cacao embriagante que tomaban,
Del tabaco aromático que aspiraban,
Y como los indios no parecían amigables,
Ordené a mis hombres que tocaran música,
Y sirvieran nuestro escaso vino
Y bailaran para invitarlos.

That burning, blinding light is like the sea
Of fire we encountered on the final
Voyage, a fire that encircled us
Belching its clouds of smoke into waves
Maddened by the wind. Or the sea of blood,
An ocean filled with reddened waters
Like a cauldron set on Satan's fires.
The blood—was it real or mere illusion?
Or was it the blood of all the Indians
Who killed themselves by hanging or by poison?
We threw their bodies into the ocean
To be torn apart by ravening sea beasts.
It was then I began to deny my God:
Malaria, fever, disease rotted my brain
And the brains of all my crew. And if
We did not forge an idol it was only
Because we never found the gold to raise one,
Though it was there beyond the enchanted isles
That wove a labyrinth around Cathay
And its domains.

                *   *   *

The bells are tolling the hour. One, two...
Five of them. Dawn is drawing near.
I can hear the uproar of the maddened waves
Breaking against the rocky cliffs. Cathay...
The Great Khan...gold...the suicides...
We sailed, not knowing where we were,
Entering seas that grew ever more dense,
More full of danger. At last we reached a shore
Covered with fruit trees, and rivers of crystal
Water, and the heady cacao the Indians
Drank, and the aromatic tobacco
They breathed in. And since the Indians seemed

Los indios pensaron que bailábamos una danza de guerra,
Y mientras nos esmerábamos en entretenerlos
Nos atacaron con flechas venenosas.
Los dardos zumbaban igual que avispas certeras,
Y así diezmaron nuestras fuerzas.
Salimos huyendo a toda prisa.
Los cadáveres sobre cubierta
Empezaron a descomponerse
Pero ya estábamos acostumbrados a la podredumbre.
Llevábamos semanas comiendo de noche
Para no ver los gusanos verdes y velludos
Que anidaban como llagas vivas
En los panes que habíamos traído de España.
Los marineros tomaron canoas y se lanzaron
A buscar la ruta de Castilla.

    *   *   *

Empecé a temer por mi vida.
Así, una noche de luna,
Pero nublada de tal manera
Que el mar sólo parecía iluminado
A pedazos—aquí la luz, allá la sombra—,
Decidí suicidarme.
Había navegado incansablemente
Sin encontrar lo que buscaba.
En la carabela se respiraba un aire putrefacto
De los muertos escondidos
En combate y enterrados en las tablas;
Los barriles de vino, ahora vacíos,
Convertidos en tumbas.
Los moribundos gemían lastimeramente,
Otros, poseídos, maldecían mi nombre
Y, desafiándome,
Se entregaban a la sodomía.

Hostile I ordered my men to play music,
And serve them the little wine we had,
And dance as an invitation to friendship.
They thought it was a war dance,
And while we took great care to entertain them
They attacked us with venom-tipped arrows
That buzzed like well-aimed wasps. They ravaged
Our forces. We fled, scrambled out of sight.
The corpses on the deck began to rot
But we had grown used to putrefaction.
For weeks we ate at night so we would not see
The greenish hairy worms like living wounds
In the loaves of bread we had brought from Spain.
The sailors set out in canoes to find
The route back to Castille.

*   *   *

I began to fear for my life.
One moonlit cloudy night when the sea
Seemed illumined patchwork—light here, there shadow—
I determined to take my own life.
I had sailed unceasingly yet never found
What I was searching for. The caravelle
Smelled of rotting bodies
Hidden under the boards in combat. The casks
Of wine were emptied now, turned into tombs.
The dying moaned; the others, possessed, cursed
My name, and in defiance of my orders
Turned again to sodomy.
I went to my cabin, lit the lamp,
And sat to write an entry in my diary.
For the first time ever my mind was blank.
The words clutched at my brain and would not let
My soul touch them. I wanted to devise

Fuí a mi cabina, prendí la lámpara
Y me senté a escribir en el Diario.
Por primera vez
Tenía la mente en blanco.
Las palabras se aferraban a mi cerebro
Sin dejar que las tocara el alma.
Me hubiera gustado inventar un nuevo lenguaje
Para describir este mundo de maldiciones
Y no de maravillas.
Los mosquitos zumbaban enervados
Alrededor de mi cabeza.
Afuera soplaba una leve brisa,
Pero dentro de la cabina
Todo era sofocación y muerte.
Invoqué el espíritu de Dios como único guía.
El silencio fue la respuesta.
Me arodillé en el suelo tambaleante
Y oré con mis manos aferradas,
Los ojos cerrados,
El corazón oprimido.
Oré desnudando mi alma de toda vanidad
Y pedí una señal, una luz,
Un fin a mi suplicio.
Me despojé de mis vestimentas
Y salí sin ser visto
Para lanzarme a las aguas,
No para llegar a ninguna costa,
Sino para desaparecer ahogado;
Para ser despedazado por las bestias,
Para que de mi cuerpo no quedara rastro,
Ni vestigio alguno.
El agua estaba cálida. Me sumergí
Buscando un camino hacia las profundidades.
En ese instante se abrió una brecha entre las nubes,
La luna brilló y mostró

A new language to describe
This world of maledictions, not marvels.
Crazed mosquitoes careened around my head.
Outside a light breeze blew, but in the cabin
Were only airlessness and death. I invoked
The Spirit of God as my guide. The response
Was silence. I fell to my knees, to the rocking floor,
And prayed, hands clasped, eyes closed, heart oppressed.
I prayed, stripping my soul of vanity,
And begged for a sign, a light, an end
To my anguish. I undressed and went to the deck,
Unseen, to plunge into the water,
Not to swim to land but to drown, to disappear,
Torn to pieces by the beasts, leaving no trace,
No vestige of my body. I leaped; the
Water was warm. I was searching for the route
Down to the depths. When the clouds moved away
From the moon, its light revealed to my eyes
A strange, dense element. I swam
With all my strength, attempting to touch that
Perfect circle on the sea floor like a great gold coin
Waiting for my grasp. Then I knew that life
Still mattered to me, for I could feel desire.
I wanted to say a prayer of thanksgiving
But a silvery wave swept me away
Flooding my eyes with lights, with stars, while my heart
Pounded with the miracle of new life.

    *   *   *

I opened my eyes, gasping on an unknown shore.
The flickering lamps of the fireflies
Lit the strand. My forces spent, I could not recognize
This place I'd been brought to. I tried
To penetrate its meaning as I watched

El elemento extraño e impenetrable.
Nadé con fuerza, buscando
La circunferencia perfecta en el fondo
Como si fuera una inmensa moneda de oro
Esperando ser rescatada.
Comprendí que todavía
Me importaba la vida pues era
Capaz de experimentar el deseo.
En ese instante quise dar Gracias
Más una ola plateada me arrastró,
Inundando mis ojos de luces, de estrellas,
Mientras mi corazón pulsaba
Ante el milagro de la nueva vida.

     *   *   *

Al abrir los ojos
Me encontré en una costa extraña.
Estaba sin aliento. Las luciérnagas
Eran lámparas fugaces iluminando
El espectáculo. Sin fuerzas,
Tratando de reconocer el paraje
Sobre el cual había sido depositado,
Y tratando de descifrar el mensaje,
Vi los cangrejos a la luz de la luna,
Corriendo de hueco en hueco,
Alarmados ante el intruso
Que violaba sus moradas.
Oí un rumor de plumas,
De objetos de oro que hacían música en el viento,
Y luego vi unos toscos pies acercándose.
Levanté el rostro. Descubrí
Un anciano cacique indígena
Bronceado como una almendra
De cabellos color de huesos viejos y pulidos,

Crabs in the moonlight scuttling from hole to hole,
Terrified by the intruder
Who'd violated their home. I heard
The whisper of feathers, the music of
Gold objects in the breeze, and then I saw
Rough feet walking toward me. I raised my head:
I saw an ancient Indian chieftain
Sun-browned as an almond,
His hair the color of old polished bones,
His hands bearing a lance.
His eyes burned in the darkness.
For a moment I feared I would end my days
Between the jaws of a cannibal,
But he was somehow incorporeal,
His substance transformed. The old man took my hand
And I, astounded, rose to my knees
And then my feet. We walked away from the shore.
In the distance, on the onyx water,
We could see the lights of the carvelles.
And yet I felt no wish to return, I longed
To move beyond, to find the new,
The undiscovered. The old man
Was no spirit, no cannibal, no astute
Envoy of the Great Khan. He was a wizard,
A magician. He led me to his hut
And said: "It is a great sin, My Lord,
To attempt to limit the soul, to humble it
Saying 'You can go no further'—it is like
Trying to humble God. For you, who halted
The moon in its path, are a great wizard,
The only immortal of all the cruel invaders…"

             *   *   *

When the curtains of heaven began to part

Arrstrando una lanza en sus manos.
En la oscuridad
sus ojos brillaban, encendidos.
Por un momento sentí pavor de acabar mi vida
En las mandíbulas de un caníbal,
Pero este hombre era inmaterial
Como si estuviese transubstanciado.
El anciano tomó mi mano, y yo, maravillado,
Me puse de rodillas y luego de pies.
Nos alejamos de la orilla.
A lo lejos, sobre la superficie ónix se veían
Las luces de las carabelas. Y sin embargo
No sentía deseos de regresar,
Sino de seguir adelante,
De encontrar algo diferente
A todo lo que había descubierto.
El hombre no era un espíritu, ni un caníbal.
Tampoco era un sabio mensajero del Gran Khan,
Sino un mago, un brujo.
Me condujo a su cabaña y me dijo:
"Gran pecado es, Majestad,
Poner límites al alma—humillarla y decirle:
No puedes ir más allá—es como humillar a Dios.
Pues tú, que detuviste la luna,
Eres el gran mago, el único inmortal
Entre los crueles invasores...".

      *   *   *

Cuando la corredera del cielo
Se abría en el horizonte
Y las estrellas se desprendían fugazmente
De la carpa violácea para ocultarse en el Atlántico,
El anciano me acompañó haste la playa.
Besé su mano y miré por última vez su rostro.

On the horizon, and the fleeting stars
Dropped from the violet canopy to hide
In the Atlantic, the old man led me
Back to the beach. I kissed his hand
And looked for the last time upon his face.
Then I plunged into the water once again
And the same silvery wave that carried me
To the shore returned me to the ship.
Later, as the sun celebrated the rites
Of a new day, I wrote words of thanksgiving
In my diary, praises to the Lord
And his loving kindness. The next morning,
When the anchors were weighed again,
We came upon a monstrous whirlpool racing
Toward our caravelle to gulp it down.
The sailors were struck with panic; they spoke
Of sacrificing me to the Wrath of God.
I remembered my pact with Our Lord whom I
Had denied hours before, I recalled
The noble mission that had been given me,
And I took the Holy Bible in my hand
And read aloud from Scripture as I traced
A circle in the air with my sword,
And I watched the whirlpool vanish while my heart
Shuddered. I heard the voice I had longed for:
"Oh man of little faith, do not be afraid,
It is I. Have courage, do not falter,
Do not allow fear to triumph. The seven
Years granted for finding gold are not yet
Accomplished, and in that promise, in all
The promises I have made to you,
I will not abandon you,
For you are one of my chosen."

    *   *   *

Me sumergí en las aguas, y la misma
Ola plateada que me había conducido
Hasta la orilla, me depositó en el barco.
Más tarde, mientras el sol
Celebraba las ceremonias de un nuevo día,
Escribí en mi diario palabras
De Gracias, Loas al Señor y sus bondades.
La mañana siguiente, levantadas las anclas,
Encontramos un molino de agua
Dirigiéndose hacia nuestra carabela para engullirla.
Los marineros, dominados por el pánico,
Hablaron de sacrificarme a la Ira Divina.
Recordé en ese instante mi pacto con Dios
De quien unas horas antes había renegado,
Recordé la grandeza de la misión
Que se me había encomendado,
Tomé la *Biblia*, leí del Evangelio,
Y trazando un círculo con mi espada
Vi el molino desvaneciéndose
Mientras mi corazón se estremecía.
Escuché la voz anhelada:
"Hombre de poca Fe, no temas, soy yo.
Ten coraje; no desmayes,
No permitas que el miedo triunfe.
Los siete años de límite para encontrar
El oro no se han vencido,
Y en esa promesa, como en todas las que te hecho,
No te abandonaré pues eres mi escogido".

        *   *   *

¡Tengo que descubrir el oro!
¡Tengo que liberar a Jerusalém de los paganos!
¡Tengo que ayudar a mi pueblo a cruzar el océano!
Escucho a los gallos cantar. Como Pedro,

I must find gold! I must free Jerusalem
From the infidels! I must
Help my people to cross the ocean sea!
I hear the roosters crowing. Like Peter,
I too denied Christ.
The priest is here. Why does he bring incense?
Why does he bend over me and give his blessings?
Why does he place the sacred host on my forehead
And make the sign of the cross? Let them
Remove the chains from under my bed
And lock them round my ankles and wrists!
These are the irons I dragged from town to town;
They cut my hands and feet, left open wounds.
Yes, my spirit is free and knows no bounds,
But like Christ crucified
I want to die in chains
So that men will always remember greed
And the barriers raised by envy. Hold
My body to the bed! My soul is rising!
Someone has opened the windows. I see
An ocean, not the everyday faces,
The horror of yet another voyage
Into the unknown, into the naked kingdoms
Of my trembling heart. Oh Thou, Hand of Fire
Te Deum laudamus...
All seas crossed, all peninsulas explored,
The voyage ended in a dying wave
Facing its destiny,
In manes tuas, Domine
Commendo Spiritum Meum.

Medellín, Quirama, 1979

Yo también renegué de Cristo.
Ese es el cura. ¿Por qué el incienso?
¿Por qué se inclina sobre mí y me bendice?
¿Por qué coloca la hostia sagrada sobre
Mi frente y hace la señal de la cruz?
Saquen las cadenas debajo de mi cama—
¡Ajústenlas a mis manos y tobillos!
Esos hierros que he cargado de pueblo en pueblo,
Cicatrizándome las manos y los pies
Y cubriéndolos de llagas.
Sí, mi espíritu está libre
Y desconoce las fronteras.
Como Cristo en su cruz
Quiero morir encadenado
Para recordarle a los hombres
La avaricia y las barreras
Que la envidia cultiva.
¡Aferren mi cuerpo al lecho
Porque en este instante mi alma se eleva!
Alguien abre las ventanas.
Veo un mar y no los rostros de siempre,
Y el horror de otro viaje desconocido
Hacia reinos desnudos en el corazón estremecido.
Oh tú, Mano de Fuego,
Te Deum laudamus
Cruzados los mares,
exploradas las penínsulas,
Terminado el viaje,
Como una ola agotada
Que encuentra su destino,
In manes tuas, Domine
Comendo Spiritum Meum.

Medellín, Quirama, 1979

ACKNOWLEDGMENTS

Poems previously published in English are "Baudelaire's Spleen," *WV*, Vol. 1, 1998; and in *The World in Us*, edited by Michael Lassell and Elena Georgiou (St. Martin's Press), New York, N.Y., 2000; "Tarzan" in *The World in Us*; "Leaving Ybor City," in *Word of Mouth*, edited by Timothy Liu (Talisman House), Jersey City, N.J., 2000 and in *Barrio Streets Carnival Dreams*, edited by Lori Marie Carlson (Henry Holt and Company), New York, N.Y., 1996. "Poem for Matthew Shepard," *Blood & Tears,* edited by Scott Gibson (Painted Leaf Press), New York, N.Y. 1999.

All the poems included in Part One previously appeared in the volume *Mi cuerpo y otros poemas*, Casa Silva (Bogotá, Colombia), 1999.

My thanks to Instituto Quirama, outside Medellín, Colombia, where *Christopher Columbus: Reflections on His Deathbed* was written; to my extraordinary translators, Edith Grossman and Margaret Sayers Peden; to the Foundation for the Performance of the Contemporary Arts, for a grant that gave me the impetus to start gathering the materials in this manuscript; to the John Simon Guggenheim Memorial Foundation, for a fellowship that freed my time to give my undivided attention to arranging and putting the final touches on this volume; and finally, to Bill Sullivan, Publisher of Painted Leaf Press, for his belief in my poetry.

About The Author

JAIME MANRIQUE was born in Colombia. His work has been translated into many languages. Mr. Manrique reviews for *Salon.com* and the *Washington Post Book World,* and teaches in the MFA program at Columbia University, and at Eugene Lang College of the New School. Among his honors are Colombia's National Poetry Award, grants from the Foundation for Contemporary Performance Arts, the New York Foundation for the Arts, and a Guggenheim fellowship in 2000.

Photo: Star Black

About the Translators

EDITH GROSSMAN, celebrated for her translations of the work of Gabriel García Márquez, Mario Vargas Llosa, Alvaro Mutis, and Mayra Montero, among others, is recognized as one of the most distinguished translators of Latin American literature in our time. She is currently working on a new translation of *Don Quixote.*

MARGARET SAYERS PEDEN lives in Columbia, Missouri. Among her highly regarded and honored translations are the works of Pablo Neruda, Octavio Paz, Sor Juana Inés de la Cruz, Juan Rulfo, and José Emilio Pacheco. Her most recent publications include Isabel Allende's *Paula, Aphrodite,* and *Daughter of Fortune.*